FOREIGN ACQUISITIONS
AND THE SPREAD
OF THE MULTINATIONAL FIRM

*This is a volume
in the Arno Press collection*

MULTINATIONAL CORPORATIONS:
Operations and Finance

Advisory Editor
Stuart Bruchey

*See last pages of this volume
for a complete list of titles*

FOREIGN ACQUISITIONS
AND THE SPREAD
OF THE MULTINATIONAL FIRM

Michael Dubin

ARNO PRESS
A New York Times Company
New York • 1980

Editorial Supervision: Erin Foley

First Publication 1980 by Arno Press Inc.

MULTINATIONAL CORPORATIONS: Operations and Finance
ISBN for complete set: 0-405-13350-2
See last pages of this volume for titles.

Manufactured in the United States of America

Library of Congress Cataloging in Publication Data

Dubin, Michael.
   Foreign acquisitions and the spread of the multinational firm.

   (Multinational corporations)
   Originally presented as the author's thesis,
Harvard.
   1. Corporations, Foreign. 2. International
business enterprises. 3. Investments, Foreign.
I. Title. II. Series.
HD2755.5.D83   1980   338.8'81   80-572
ISBN 0-405-13366-9
HG4027.5.H44 1980   658.1'52   80-575
ISBN 0-405-13368-5

Foreign Acquisitions

and the Spread of the Multinational Firm

Michael Dubin

A thesis submitted in partial fulfillment
of the requirements for the degree of
Doctor of Business Administration

Graduate School of Business Administration
George F. Baker Foundation
Harvard University

ABSTRACT

Foreign Acquisitions and the Spread of the Multinational Firm

Michael Dubin

While the behavior of multinational firms has been extensively researched in recent years, little substantive conceptual foundation has been laid for cross-border acquisitions, particularly from a micro-economic point of view. The question is not unimportant as nearly fifty percent of all manufacturing subsidiaries established abroad by U.S. firms have been acquired.

This study concludes that two characteristics of acquisitions are of systematic importance in the foreign investment decision: first is the ability to reduce the perceived level of risk, and second is the capacity to effect speedy transfer to foreign operations of highly developed, but underutilized, parent skills. A broader macro-economic foundation for the behavior of multinational firms was drawn from the product life cycle model of foreign investment. Tests using close to 5,000 manufacturing subsidiaries formed since 1900 by 187 U.S.-based multinational firms were supportive of the conceptual framework.

For the total sample, the acquisition rate among foreign subsidiaries showed a generally rising trend over time, increasing sharply in the late 1960's, with some cyclical peaks and troughs corresponding to cycles in acquisition activity in the United States. The most remarkable conclusion of the study was that, acting counter to this trend, was the systematic influence of parent size on the acquisition rate. The larger and more experienced that firms became, the less frequently acquisitions were used in expanding abroad. It was the small firms, relatively inexperienced abroad, that turned actively to acquisitions. The ability of acquisitions to reduce the overall corporate risk in the foreign investment decision was a critical factor underlying this behavior.

Risk reduction was particularly evident in the role that acquisitions played during periods of follow-the-leader behavior in which U.S. firms rapidly countered the foreign moves of their U.S. competitors. The acquisition rate for most industries rose measurably above average levels during such periods.

The ability to reduce risk as well as to utilize complementarities between parent and foreign subsidiaries were important factors in explaining the effects that other parent, industry, and host country characteristics had on acquisition rates. Among the major conclusions was that diversification in foreign markets revealed a heavy reliance on acquisitions. High acquisition rates were also found in product-differentiated industries as well as in industries characterized by high levels of instability or rapid technological change. By contrast, industries where either economies of scale were significant or concentration was high, the rate of acquisition was typically low. Various host country characteristics had a positive effect on acquisitions, namely large market size, high rate of real growth, and cultural or locational proximity to the United States.

The results suggest that managers calculations ex ante are consistent with a profit-maximizing view of the firm, rather than alternative behavioral models, such as growth maximization. A worldwide view of the parent system that enables the decision maker to measure the marginal impact of an incremental investment on the system's overall risk and return is essential to evaluating foreign acquisition decisions. Various prospects and pitfalls facing the acquisition decision are discussed. The implications for host country policies include the potential to design incentive schemes using selective accessibility to acquisitions of local firms as a means of encouraging foreign investment.

Table of Contents

I. Introduction

This is a study of foreign expansion through acquisition. Nearly fifty percent of U.S. manufacturing subsidiaries established abroad since the beginning of the twentieth century have been acquisitions. The trend of foreign acquisition activity well into the late 1960's has been on the increase. This study examines the attributes of acquisitions that lie behind this active role in the foreign investment process.

The initial interest in this study was derived from the broad ground work laid by the research effort on U.S.-based multinational firms directed by Professor Raymond Vernon. These studies helped to identify patterns in the behavior of large multinational firms--in terms of strategy, structure, ownership, and functional characteristics. Little systematic attention, however, was given to the subject of acquisitions. While various aspects of the timing of entry into foreign markets were closely examined, the choice of a method of entry (acquisition vs. de novo investment) was not explored. Moreover, in spite of the fact that the rapid growth in the number of foreign acquisitions of U.S. multinational firms has attracted a great deal of public attention, the evidence on the behavior of firms in making acquisitions across national borders has been skimpy. This

is even more surprising in view of the extensive literature
on acquisition activity in domestic settings.

Data limitations have no doubt contributed to the
lack of research in this area. Detailed financial data is
difficult to obtain; the original design of the large
sample of data collected in the Vernon study did not regard
the collection of financial data as feasible. Nevertheless,
the data on the overall flow of acquisitions was more than
sufficient to extract a number of simple but valuable conclusions about the role of acquisitions in foreign direct
investment.

A Preview of the Patterns in Foreign Acquisitions.
The attractiveness of foreign acquisitions has waxed and
waned since the turn of the century, although there has been
a rather steady upward trend in the percentage of acquisitions among new subsidiaries formed abroad. On top of this
rising secular trend, cycles of overseas acquisition activity
were observed to be partially coincidental with cycles of
merger activity in the United States. Since the end of
World War II, the rate of foreign acquisitions has increased
manyfold, with particularly heavy interest in the 1960's.

This study shows that the overall cycles of acquisition
activity disguise several divergent trends. The patterns
of acquisitions become more understandable upon examining
several cross-currents of influence, resulting from variations

in parent, industry and host country characteristics.

Parent size appeared to be the most important systematic
influence on the rate of foreign acquisitions. In general,
the larger the parent firm and the longer its accumulated
experience in foreign markets, the less frequently acquisitions were used as a means of establishing foreign operations.
Firms that were small and relatively inexperienced in foreign
countries leaned more heavily on acquisitions, apparently as
a means of reducing the high risk of entry into foreign
markets.

It might appear as a bit of a paradox that while the
overall frequency of acquisitions was clearly rising over
the last few decades, the larger firms were gradually turning
away from acquisitions. The entry of new firms to the
foreign field over this same period was a primary cause for
the steady increase in the overall percentage of acquisitions.

The tendency for firms to diversify their operations in
foreign markets appeared to go hand-in-hand with an increasing
preference for foreign acquisitions. Significant diversification by U.S. firms overseas was not uncommon, although
foreign diversification clearly lagged its appearance in
U.S. markets.

Industry influences were also strong. High levels of
acquisition activity appeared in industries characterized by
relatively high levels of instability resulting either from
a high rate of inflow of U.S. parents into a foreign industry

or rapid technological change within the industry. Particularly industries with high levels of product differentiation, but specifically in those industries where there was an ability to spread highly developed core skills over multiple plant facilities, were accompanied by high rates of acquisition.

Host countries with high levels of economic development provided a natural magnet for acquisitions, as did countries with above average growth rates. Cultural and locational proximity to the United States were particularly attractive outlets for acquisition activity by small parent firms, presumably intent on reducing risk.

Over certain periods of time, firms in selected industries exhibited a strong follow-the-leader behavior in the timing of their investment decisions. This kind of competitive reaction, a process often referred to as defensive investment, involved a heavy use of acquisitions. The ability of acquisitions to provide a firm with quick access to new markets reduced the level of risk of investing abroad during those periods when investments in similar markets were being undertaken by competing multinationals.

Key Factors in the Attractiveness of Acquisitions. Running through the major conclusions of the study were common threads that appeared to make acquisitions more attractive to the potential foreign investor than alternative means of serving foreign markets--such as starting a new

subsidiary from scratch, expanding an existing facility,
licensing a foreign company, or continuing to export from
the parent's home country. In a review of the theory of
acquisitions to determine the attractiveness of acquisitions in foreign markets, several factors stood out in
importance: the ability of acquisitions to serve as a
vehicle for implementing risk-avoidance strategies and the
capacity of acquisitions to function as a conduit for
exploiting highly developed parent skills.

Risk reduction was a goal given high priority in the
foreign direct investment process. As a first stepping
stone into new markets or as a means by which rapid reaction
to competitors moves can be accomplished, acquisitions
appear to play a vital role in reducing the risk of investing
abroad. The risk-avoidance reaction also appears to lead
to greater use of acquisitions during periods of instability
and rapid technological change.

The ability to transmit key human skills from the
parent to foreign markets constituted a second major attri-
bute of acquisitions. Acquisitions were particularly
valuable for situations where the marginal cost of an
outbound transfer of core skills was low and the potential
margin return in foreign markets was high.

Fitting the Attributes of Acquisitions into a Model
of Foreign Investment. In order to show that these characteristics of acquisitions were significant to the foreign

investment process, their setting had to be identified in terms of a general model of the behavior of multinational firms. Only after examining what motivated U.S. firms to invest in foreign markets could the importance of the role of acquisitions as a tool for risk reduction and transfer of skills be placed in proper perspective.

The product life cycle model of foreign direct investment,[1] sets out the underlying factors that led U.S. firms through a sequence of steps starting with the development of a domestic foundation of complex technologies, products, production methods and skills and leading to the eventual investment in productive facilities in foreign markets. The internationalization of these enterprises typically evolved in industries characterized by oligopolistic structures. The behavior of firms in oligopolies is noted for the high priority given to such factors as the reduction of risk tied in strongly with the use of acquisitions during specific periods of time.

Summary of What is to Come. It is in the context of the product life cycle development of the foreign side of U.S. enterprise that acquisitions take on their significance. Following a brief review of the methodology and data, a discussion of the product life cycle theory sets the stage for a more thorough look at the nature of acquisitions and their role in overseas investment. Then, the analysis

Then, the analysis turns to the underlying structural
factors that affect acquisition rates. Reviewed are the
significant parent, industry and host country characteristics
felt to be determinants of rates of acquisition. The
special focus of the final part of the study is on the
active role acquisitions played during the intensive periods
of follow-the-leader behavior.

FOOTNOTES TO CHAPTER 1

[1]
Raymond Vernon, "International Investment and International Trade in the Product Cycle," Quarterly Journal of Economics, May 1966, pp. 190-207.

II. Methodology and Data

The objective of the thesis was to show significant trends and patterns in foreign acquisitions by U.S. multinationals. These patterns were typically analyzed by looking at the number of foreign acquisitions formed annually since 1900 by major firms. The measures of acquisitions used were simple: either the number of acquisitions or the percentage of subsidiaries formed by acquisition in a given period was most frequently used as the dependent variable. In the sections dealing with acquisitions during periods of concentrated bunching at entry, a somewhat more abstract measure (referred to as an Entry Concentration Index or ECI) was used to determine the time periods in which acquisition activity was to be measured. The construction of the ECI is discussed in Chapter XI.

The data used to test the hypotheses of the study came from various sources. The data on foreign subsidiaries came from data collected by Professor Raymond Vernon in his study of multinational firms. Data for U.S. parent firms came from many sources, most of which were public; but some of which were collected by other researchers at the Harvard Business School--in particular, Professor Jesse W. Markham's Large Diversified Firm data base.

Multinational Enterprise Data Base

The data on which most statistical tests were made
came from the Multinational Enterprise Data Base developed
by Professor Raymond Vernon at the Harvard Business School.
This data base contained information on over 11,000 subsidiaries of 187 parent firms that were defined by the Vernon
study as being U.S.-based multinational firms--those that
appeared on the Fortune 500 in 1964 or 1965 and had manufacturing subsidiaries in six or more countries. Nearly
the entire history of foreign expansion of these enterprises
up until 1967 was contained in the data. Close to half
(nearly 5,000) of the subsidiaries were formed through
acquisition.

Variables Available. The data base contained close to
100 pieces of information on each subsidiary. However, for
the purposes of this study, the key variables of interest
were those that related to the characteristics of the subsidiary at the time of entry (and exit) as well as subsequent changes in its product mix. Among the variables
analyzed were: the nation in which manufacturing occurred;
the year of entry of the subsidiary into the parent system;
the method of entry (e.g., acquisition); the name of the
parent; the products produced at entry (according to the
3-digit SIC classification); the products produced in 1966;
and for some subsidiaries, the products produced at the date

when manufacturing began. Unfortunately, little or no data
was consistently available on the size of the subsidiaries
acquired or on financial characteristics of the subsidiaries.

Data on Manufacturing Subsidiaries

Since the tests for a number of the hypotheses of
the study related largely to industry characteristics, it
was only possible to use observations on which 3-digit SIC
product classifications were available. Such information had
been gathered primarily for manufacturing subsidiaries and
not for subsidiaries engaged in extractive operations, sales
or other operations. The total number of subsidiaries
engaged in manufacturing at some time before 1967 was
slightly over 5,200; approximately half of which were
acquired.

Subsets of Time Periods, Countries and Industries.
For most of the tests this entire sample of data on manufacturing subsidiaries was employed, as the objective of
the tests was to observe the general pattern of acquisition and direct investment flows. For a limited series of
tests, various sub-samples of data were used. There were
two primary reasons for breaking down the data into
smaller subsets: first, there was a need to exclude time
periods, industries and countries that had only a small
number of manufacturing subsidiaries; second, there was
a specific interest in the post-war period for major industries and countries in order to complement and extend

existing literature on foreign direct investment (and particularly foreign takeovers) which has largely been confined
to the post-war period. Furthermore, little hard data
existed for many of the variables of interest in this study
for the time period before World War II.

In particular, the latter part of the thesis, dealing
with defensive acquisitions during the periods of oligopolistic reaction, was confined exclusively to the data in the
post-war period. The subset of data used most often as an
alternative to the whole data base is described below.

1. Time Period: 1948-1967. The two years immediately
following the end of World War II were also eliminated
because of the possible distortions in activity that may
have resulted from immediate post-war adjustments. This
subset of data thus spanned the period from 1948 through
1967 inclusive. Over 75% of all subsidiaries that ever
began manufacturing did so after 1947. This period, as
well as a number of other restrictions on the data, was
similar to that used in the Knickerbocker study,[1] making
these results complementary to the extent possible.

2. Countries. Out of a possible 149 countries,
only those that contained a large enough number of subsidiaries to construct the appropriate measures of acquisition
activity (described in detail later) were selected for the

subset of data. Canada was also excluded because of its
close relationship to the U.S. market. In the eyes of most
multinational firms investments in Canada would be made partially on the basis of factors not considered in this study.
A total of 23 countries was finally selected; however they
accounted for over 83% of the total number of manufacturing
subsidiaries (excluding Canadian operations). The 23 countries included the original six EEC countries (France,
Germany, Italy, Belgium, The Netherlands, Luxemburg); three
other European countries (United Kingdom, Switzerland, Spain);
three Scandinavian countries (Denmark, Norway, Sweden); six
Latin American countries (Argentina, Brazil, Colombia,
Mexico, Peru, Venezuela); and five other countries (Japan,
The Philippines, Australia, New Zealand, South Africa).

     3. Industries. Out of a total of 152 3-digit SIC
industries in which subsidiaries manufactured products, 55
were finally selected for the subsets. Again only those
3-digit SIC industries that had enough subsidiaries to
calculate a meaningful measure of acquisition activity were
retained for the study. In some of the analytical parts of
the study, as few as 22 industries were used because of the
problem of the small size of the number of observations in
some industries.

4. Classification of Subsidiaries by Industry. Each
subsidiary was classified according to the 3-digit SIC
industry of the product (or products) it produced at the
time of entry. If a subsidiary manufactured more than one
product at the time of entry, the subsidiary was included
on the industry lists of each of the industries in which it
produced a product.

Data Sources for Parent, Industry and Host Country Characteristics

Various sources of data were used including data
bases complied by researchers at the Harvard Business School
as well as data from public sources.

Multinational Enterprise Data Base on Parent Firms. A
separate data base was complied for the 187 parent firms
identified as being multinational for Professor Vernon's
study. Most of the measures of the parent characteristics
came from the Standard and Poors Compustat tape service in
1966 and the Fortune Plant and Product Directory 1966, with
the exception of R&D and advertising expenditure-to-sales
ratios which came from News Front.[2] Product classifications
were based on the Standard Industrial Classification Manual
published in 1967 by the U.S. Technical Committee on
Industrial Classification.

Diversified Firm Data Base. Additional parent firm
data specifically relating to acquisitions came from the Large
Diversified Firm data base developed by Professor Jesse W.
Markham at the Harvard Business School in connection with
his study of conglomerate merger activity in the United
States. The data base included a large number of variables
developed from questionnaire results, other variables from
published sources, and a few taken from the Multinational
Enterprise Data Bank. This data base was relevant to this
study because of its potential to relate domestic acquisition behavior to foreign acquisition behavior of the same
firms.

Other Data on Industry and Host Country Characteristics.
With the exception of the two Harvard Business School data
bases, the rest of the data was taken from public sources
and are referred to in greater detail in the sections in
which the data is examined. In particular, the measures of
industry concentration ratios;[3] industry R&D expenditures;[4]
industry advertising expenditures;[5] and various measures of
scale economies[6] were taken from U.S. government publications.
Host country characteristics were taken from various international sources.[7]

Limitations of the Study. While the study purports to
show a large amount of statistical support for the relationship between various factors (such as parent size) and the
rate of acquisition, there is always the lurking question of

causality that is hard to grapple with. Causality cannot be proved, of course. Only an accumulation of evidence in favor of the relationships shown can lead to acceptance of the validity of the hypothesized direction of causality. The attempt to use correlation analysis to distinguish the causal relationships gave some indications as to the direction and significance of the indicators hypothesized, but more specific tests using data with greater levels of disaggregation would be more satisfying.

As an indication of some of the limitations of the study, the nature of the data base provided some clear illustrations. First, there was no indication of the dollar value of acquisitions, only the number of acquisitions. This would lead to bias for years or for industries where the typical size of subsidiaries acquired differed from the average. A rough check both by time and, to a lesser extent, by industry was available in terms of the total value of acquisitions, as opposed to the number, over selected time periods and for some industries in individual countries. In general, the patterns by dollar value and by number were similar.

A somewhat similar study of U.S. acquisition patterns, again by numbers, conducted by Booz, Allen and Hamilton also showed basically similar overall patterns in foreign acquisitions by U.S. multinationals.[8]

An analysis based on the value of acquisitions
rather than the number of acquisitions might produce different results in the section on parent size, if in fact
larger firms owned larger subsidiaries than smaller firms.
The results of the current analysis, however, would have
only been emphasized more strongly in the same direction.

Among other areas of potential bias, the method
of classification of subsidiaries according to the industry
of manufacture ought to be mentioned. When a subsidiary
produced more than one product, the subsidiary was recorded
as a statistic in the separate analysis of each of the
3-digit industries. Thus, a subsidiary that produced three
products at the time of its entry (the maximum for any one
subsidiary was five) would show up as a separate subsidiary
in each of the three industry categories. However, as the
number of multi-product subsidiaries that were acquired was
approximately the same order of magnitude as the number of
multi-product subsidiaries that were started from scratch,
little unusual bias appears to be introduced from this factor.
The breakdown of subsidiaries into product-subsidiaries were
used only in the tests in the latter part of the study that
dealt with defensive acquisitions.

While there were clearly additional limitations of
the study due to the lack of financial data, as well as the
inherent potential problems of misclassification in the basic
data, the approach used in this study was one of demonstrating

broad-based and systematic evidence in support of the
major hypotheses, without trying to wrench a high level of
statistical accuracy that might be subject to question on
the basis of uncertainties in the underlying data.

Outline of the Study

The first half of the study, in fact the majority of
the study, examines the broader causal factors that have led
to the use of foreign acquisitions in the process of overseas
direct investment. Analysis of the characteristics of the
flow of investment overseas via the product life cycle
model (Chapter III) sets the stage on which the attributes of
acquisitions are examined for their usefulness (Chapter IV).

Various factors are examined to see if the model
developed for the role of acquisitions in foreign investment
is consistent with its predictions. First the influence of
parent characteristics, particularly parent size (Chapter V),
is tested. Expecting that industry characteristics will
exert some independent influences of their own on acquisition
rates, their effects are tested (Chapters VII and VIII).
Host country characteristics are not neglected (Chapter IX).

A separate, and even more active, role was expected
for acquisitions during the periods of oligopolistic reaction,
or bunching of subsidiaries at entry (Chapters X to XII).

FOOTNOTES TO CHAPTER II

[1]
F. T. Knickerbocker, Oligopolistic Reaction and Multinational Enterprise (Boston: Harvard Business School, 1973).

[2]
These were obtained from various issues of News Front as noted in J. W. Vaupel and J. P. Curhan, The Making of Multinational Enterprise (Boston: Division of Research, Harvard Business School, 1969), p. 5.

[3]
U.S. Senate, Subcommittee on Antitrust and Monopoly of the Committee of the Judiciary, Concentration Ratios in Manufacturing Industry 1963 89th Congress, 2nd session, 1966.

[4]
National Science Foundation, Research and Development in Industry, 1967 (Washington: Government Printing Office, 1969).

[5]
Internal Revenue Service, Corporation Income Tax Returns: With Accounting Periods Ended July 1960-June 1961 (Washington: Government Printing Office, 1963).

[6]
U.S. Department of Commerce, Bureau of the Census, 1963 Census of Manufactures, Vol. II, Industry Statistics.

[7]
In particular, United Nations, Statistical Yearbook, 1968.

[8]
"What U.S. Companies are Doing Abroad: A Statistical Summary (prepared in cooperation with Booz, Allen & Hamilton, Inc.)," Business Abroad, May 1969, p. 13.

III. Acquisitions in the Context of the Product Life
Cycle Model and Oligopoly Theory

The basic issue under examination is the role that
acquisitions played in the process of U.S. foreign direct
investments. The first step toward an understanding of
that role is to establish certain notions about what led
U.S. firms to invest overseas. Once the motivations of
these firms are in clearer focus, our attention can be
turned to the special characteristics of acquisitions
that were relevant to the foreign investor's needs.

While various conceptual approaches have been
developed to explain the patterns of U.S. foreign direct
investment, the product life cycle model has been shown
to be very effective in describing the foreign investment
process, particularly through its ability to tie in with
oligopoly theory.[1] Understanding why multinational firms
typically inhabit oligopolistically structured industries
is key to the discussion of the role that acquisitions
have played in overseas investment. This study thus
attempts to build an additional dimension to the expana-
tory power of the product life cycle model of foreign
direct investment.

Product Life Cycle Model. Basically the product
life cycle develops a set of concepts for understanding

what led firms to turn their orientation away from the
U.S. domestic market to foreign markets. U.S. firms
back in the nineteenth century responded primarily to
the particular needs of domestic market. However, as
the particular set of conditions that characterized
U.S. markets subsequently began to appear in other major
economies, U.S. firms responded to this foreign demand
initially through exports and subsequently via direct
manufacturing facilities in foreign countries.

The initial set of conditions in the U.S. market
to which these firms responded was the existence of a
dearth of skilled labor and a large and relatively well-
off population. The United States was also blessed with
a relatively well-endowed set of natural resources. U.S.
firms were driven to innovate products and methods of
production that could both serve a large population and
at the same time not require skilled labor. Methods of
mass production were devised so that high productivity
could be achieved with unskilled labor. In addition to
innovations in mass production processes, new kinds of
skills were developed, such as an ability to make effective use of research and development to meet new market
needs, knowledge of how to bring innovations into the
market place, organizational structures to operate
efficiently in and to coordinate between many different

locations, and the capability to market on a mass scale
with flexibility to respond to the changing needs of its
customers.

These highly developed capabilities provided a base
upon which U.S. firms were later to expand overseas. On
the other hand, initially few foreign producers could
match these skills and thus were not attracted to the U.S.
market. As long as the requirements of the different
markets had little in common, the prospects for profitable
ventures across foreign borders appeared too risky.
However, as developments in foreign markets eventually
began to parallel those seen earlier in the United States,
attractive outlets for U.S. exports were created. Conditions in foreign markets began to reflect greater
scarcity in skilled labor, increasing market size, and
rising income levels. These markets began to demand the
kinds of products that U.S. firms had been producing for
domestic consumption.

However, U.S. export products eventually became
more standardized and foreign nationals began to copy
U.S. methods of production. Even though foreign producers
were at a disadvantage in terms of economies of scale,
they had the advantage of lower local cost structures,
lower transportation costs, and no tariff barriers.

Faced with the potential loss of markets, U.S. producers took the risky step of investing overseas. Armed with, among many factors, the well-developed core of parent skills that were transferable to foreign markets, U.S. firms were able to maintain a competitive advantage over their local competitors, in spite of certain higher costs of operating in a foreign environment, such as the need to communicate over long distances with the U.S. parent. The marginal cost of shifting parent skills overseas was basically low, given that the heavy expenditures to develop these skills had been made years earlier. And, more likely than not, headquarters was not making full use of these skills in the domestic market. The ability of acquisitions to transmit quickly excess parent skills to develop foreign markets was an important factor in the role that acquisitions played in the foreign investment decision, as will be shown later.

The Importance of Oligopoly Structure to Foreign Investment Patterns. While relative costs were important to the decision of U.S. firms to invest abroad, these factors alone are not sufficient to explain important elements of U.S. foreign investments. In particular, an understanding of the frequently observed follow-the-leader pattern of U.S. firms' investments overseas has been shown to be facilitated by reference to concepts from

industrial organizations theory.[2]   As noted earlier, the
U.S. industries that have been most active in foreign
direct investment have also been typically characterized
as oligopolies.

Imperfect competition and the limited number of
firms in such oligopolies prevent any single firm from
expanding rapidly except at the expense of others. An
attempt by a particular firm to alter an existing state
of balance within the oligopoly is likely to be perceived
by rival firms as a potential threat to their positions
and is likely to generate a response in a form that
diminishes that threat. In many situations a typical
response has been one of imitating the behavior of the
firm that took the initial action; in other cases, the
knowledge by all the participants in the oligopoly that
certain kinds of actions may be countered by the other
members of the oligopoly serves in itself to deter many
possible actions in the first place.

Given the relatively uncertain nature of foreign
demand for U.S. products in the early stages of U.S.
manufacturing abroad, combined with the high cost of
obtaining information overseas, the new entrant to foreign
markets is likely to seek out alternatives that would help
reduce the level of perceived risk in a foreign direct
investment.

The emphasis on risk reduction that pervades
oligopoly behavior is one of the keys to the role that
acquisitions have played in foreign investment. In the
analysis that immediately follows, the theory of acquisitions will be reviewed in order to demonstrate how acquisitions are able to provide, among other important elements,
a capacity for risk reduction in the foreign investment
decision. The focus thus shifts directly to a theory of
acquisitions and its implications for the process of
foreign direct investors.

FOOTNOTES TO CHAPTER III

[1]
For the relationship between oligopoly and foreign invest-
ments of U.S. firms see R. E. Caves, "International Corporations:
The Industrial Economics of Foreign Investment," Economica,
February 1971, pp. 10-12; R. Vernon, Sovereignty at Bay
(New York: Basic Books, 1971), and F. T. Knickerbocker,
Oligopolistic Reaction and Multinational Enterprise (Boston:
Harvard Business School, 1973), pp. 18-23. Similar relation-
ships have been found in the United Kingdom by J. H. Dunning,
American Investment in British Manufacturing Industry, 1958,
pp. 155-171; and in Canada, by G. Rosenbluth, "The Relation
Between Foreign Control and Concentration in Canadian
Industry," Canadian Journal of Economics, vol. 3. 1970,
pp. 14-30.

[2]
Knickerbocker, op. cit.

IV. Acquisition Theory and Foreign Direct Investment

The primary motivations of the foreign investor have
been brought to the surface in the context of the product
life cycle model of multinational firm behavior. It is
yet to be shown how the characteristics of acquisitions
might satisfy the needs of the foreign investor. A review
of the basic theory of acquisitions is required in order
to identify the attributes of acquisitions that are expected
to be relevant to the foreign investor. Once the connection
has been made between the motivations of the investor and
the attributes of acquisitions, it is possible to turn to
the evidence to observe whether the data confirms the
hypothesized relationships.

The Product Life Cycle Model and Acquisition Theory.
Significant in the product life cycle analysis of multinational behavior was the emphasis placed on risk aversion.
This risk avoidance propensity developed from the highly
oligopolistic structure of the industries that moved abroad.
The examination of acquisitions points out their value as
a potential vehicle for risk minimization, particularly
during periods of considerable uncertainty.

Important among the comparative advantages that set
the stage for the flow of U.S. firms into foreign markets
was the highly developed nature of human skills. The low
cost and high returns generated from putting these capabilities to use overseas was shown to be a significant

factor in this expansion. The discussion that follows will
emphasize the appropriateness of acquisitions as a medium
for accomplishing the direct flow of human skills to foreign
operations.

To establish how acquisitions have such characteristics
is the major purpose of this chapter. A look at the theory
of acquisition reveals what draws firms to their use in
foreign investments.

Theories of Acquisition

The literature specifically dealing with cross-border
acquisitions exists in large part only of descriptive works.
Organizational and legal problems are favorite topics. When
it comes to analyzing why cross-border acquisitions occur, the
usual offering is either a shopping list of reasons or a
series of case studies.

For theoretical explanations of acquisitions, domestic
studies offer the best (and only) source. Even in the domestic
setting, the issue is not resolved very well. A wide array
of different approaches is available to explain why acquisitions
occur. To be sure, surveys of the evidence of acquisition activity over previous periods of time in one-country settings have
had some success at relating facts to a given underlying theory.[1]
Nevertheless, acquisition theorists were forced to take a new
look at the old arguments following the period of widespread
increase in conglomerate activity in the 1960's.[2]

With conflicting domestic theories, each having statistical support of its own, there is no single, unified

approach to the theory of acquisition to be applied to the
foreign setting. This creates a bit of a problem for the
analyst of foreign acquisitions trends because, with a
smaller and less reliable data base, it is not an easy task
to try to test the consequences of conflicting theories.
Nevertheless, as discussed below, the array of alternative
theories is partly reduced because of fundamental differences
between a domestic expansion and a foreign expansion.
From the theories remaining, where possible, an effort has
been made to test their relative merits. Elsewhere,
evidence presented may support a single theory without
specifically testing the alternative hypotheses.

Theories of acquisition behavior can be broadly
grouped into three major categories: those that assume that
firms are profit maximizers; those that assume that firms
are growth maximizers; and those that assume that economic
disturbances distort the "normal" evaluation process.

Firms as Profit Maximizers

Under the profit maximization assumption, the price
that the managers of the acquiring firms are willing to
pay for the acquisition will be the increase in earnings
of the two firms combined, discounted to the present.
The seller sets his price in the same fashion, by dis-
counting to the present, the value of his future earnings
stream. The fact that the price that the buyer is willing

to pay for the acquisition must be higher than the price
that the seller wants to charge, sets the basic condition
under which an acquisition will take place. Mathematically
this relationship can be presented very simply as,

$$\underset{\text{Buyer's Price}}{\underbrace{\sum_{t=0}^{\infty} \frac{(PC_B)_t - (PB_B)_t}{(1 + D_B)^t}}} > \underset{\text{Seller's Price}}{\underbrace{\sum_{t=0}^{\infty} \frac{(PS_S)_t}{(1 + D_S)^t}}}$$

Where:

PC_B = Profit of Combined firm to Buyer (for each year, t)

PB_B = Profit of Buyer's firm to Buyer

PS_S = Profit of Seller's firm to Seller

D_B = Discount rate of Buyer

D_S = Discount rate of Seller

This simple relationship between the buyer and the
seller results in two basic circumstances that can cause
an acquisition to occur. First, assuming that both the
buyer and the seller apply the same discount rates to their
earnings streams, then an acquisition can occur if the
earnings stream expected from the combined firm is greater
than the sum of the earnings streams of the two firms
separately. Second, if the sum of the earnings streams
merely equals the expected earnings stream of the combined
firm, then an acquisition can occur if the buyer has a
lower discount rate than the seller. These two conditions
can be represented mathematically. First, if the discount

rate of the buyer equals the discount rate of the seller,

#1: If, $D_B = D_S$

then an acquisition can take place only if the earnings
flows of the combined firm is greater than the sum of the
earnings flows of the two firms separately.

Then, $PC_B - PB_B > PS_S$

Thus, $PC_B > PS_S + PB_B$

Second, if the alternate condition is true, i.e.,
the earnings streams of the combined firm is equal to the
sum of the earnings streams of the two firms,

#2: If, $PC_B - PB_B = PS_S$

then an acquisition can occur only if the discount rates
of the buyer is smaller than the discount rate of the
seller, or

Then, $\dfrac{PC_B - PB_B}{1 + D_B} > \dfrac{PS_S}{1 + D_S}$

But, $\dfrac{1}{1 + D_B} > \dfrac{1}{1 + D_S}$ Since, $PC_B - PB_B = PS_S$

Thus, $D_S > D_B$

Under the first category, the present value of
the earnings stream of the combined firm will be <u>higher</u>
than the sum of the present values of the firms individually
if any one (or more) of the following results come from
the acquisition: (a) an increase in the market power of
the combined firm, (b) an increase in economies of scale,
either technical or managerial, of the combined firm,

(c) the existence of opportunities for complementarity of underutilized resources present in either (or both) the buyer or seller.

(a) Market Power. An increase in the market power of the combined firm would allow for increased earnings in the form of the higher monopoly rent built into its prices. The possibilities for creating or extending market power through foreign acquisitions may be heightened for those firms where opportunities for domestic horizontal expansion are limited by U.S. antitrust regulations. The evidence on foreign subsidiaries appears to confirm that many of the foreign subsidiaries of U.S. parents produce products in the same 3-digit SIC industries as the parent's domestic products. To the extent that such subsidiaries were acquired in foreign markets, there is the potential for increased market power.

Market power might also be expected as a motivation for making acquisitions in foreign industries that are highly concentrated. The alternative of expanding internally in a highly concentrated industry, especially in an industry where foreign demand is not growing rapidly, might result in downward pressure on prices. Acquiring into such an industry would be likely to prolong the gain in earnings resulting from the decrease in competition. In industries that have a low level of concentration, the

number of firms selling in the market would make it
unlikely that acquisitions could contribute to much of
a gain in market power. That some evidence has shown a
positive relationship between concentration and acquisitions in the U.S. market, makes it possible that similar
factors may have been at work in foreign markets.[3]

(b) Economies of Scale. An increase in the economies
of scale in any number of areas within the combined firm
could generate higher earnings because of the expanded
level of output that could be obtained from the same level
of resources. The possibility of increasing the economies
of scale in many functional areas--production, marketing,
purchasing, finance, management, and research and develop-
ment--are some of the most frequently cited benefits expected from acquisitions. Nevertheless, the opportunities
for achieving increased economies of scale through acquisitions in foreign countries would appear to have clear
limitations. In the production area, location-specific
economies of scale are not likely to increase as a result
of plants in other locations. In addition, for many of
the other areas, such as management or research and development, U.S. parents are generally well endowed and would be
seeking to apply those talents rather than acquiring
additional ones; this factor is particularly relevant to
the complementarity argument that follows below.

The situations in which economies of scale might be
expected to be an important motivation for foreign acquisitions would be cases where the U.S. parent is relatively
small (or new) in a given industry that is characterized
by high levels of scale in production. Foreign acquisitions
might also be important in industries where the efficiency
of the average firm is increasing and the average size of
the industry competitor is getting larger in order to
generate greater economies of scale. Nevertheless, studies
have indicated little benefit from this factor.[4]

(c) <u>Complementarity of Underutilized Resources</u>. One
of the more fertile areas for foreign acquisitions would be
to take advantage of underutilized resources in the U.S.
parent or in the foreign seller. The combination of two
firms in situations where underutilized resources exist in
one or both creates the potential for additional profitability being generated from these idle resources. The
distinction between this argument and the economies of
scale argument is that there does not have to be any
increase in economies of scale for the complementary
resources to generate additional earnings.

An important factor underlying the presence of the
underutilized resources is that the "excess" resources are
not usually of the kind that can be sold in the market at
a price equal to the marginal productivity of these
resources.[5] These resources are likely to have been

generated through heavy investment; in some of the perhaps less obvious cases, the investment has been in human resources. These investments are generally made in rather lumpy increments, involving substantial risk.

The areas that these resources are likely to appear in the U.S. parents are in functions that require heavy emphasis on human skills, such as management, research and development, marketing and finance.

A firm that is small within a given industry (and this would include a large firm entering a new foreign industry) would be likely to have underutilized resources in the areas of management (organization), marketing, and research and development that might combine well with a foreign company with underutilized production or distribution resources. Note that the existence of the under-utilized resources within the parent alone is sufficient to stimulate the acquisition.

In industries for which research and development resources are industry-specific, firms would be likely to seek foreign acquisitions within the same industry. The same could be said of firms with other industry-specific, human-intensive skills, such as might be the case in some marketing oriented multinationals. Nevertheless, there are probably some limitations to the ability of the parent to utilize the research and development resources across industries (i.e., being somewhat industry-specific).

Finance may also be an area where excess resources exist in the parent that can be utilized by new subsidiaries. If the parent can get cheap access to capital, compared to sources in foreign countries, then an acquisition could be a means of utilizing this resource. Some have argued that differences in capitalization rates for new capital are, in themselves, an underlying explanation of why foreign direct investment occurs, and takeovers in particular. The cheaper source of capital (due to the higher capitalization rate of the acquiring firm) is the basic advantage that firms possess in taking their efforts into foreign markets.[6]

Reduction of Risk and the Discount Rate. Returning the discussion back to the beginning of the section on profit maximizing firms, the focus turns to the second condition under which acquisitions can occur. Assuming that the earnings stream of the combined firm is exactly equal to the sum of the earnings streams of the buyer and the seller independently, an acquisition can take place if the discount rate applied by the buyer to the same earnings stream is lower than that applied by the seller. A primary reason why the buyer would apply a lower discount rate would be that the buyer perceived a reduction in the overall risk in the combined firm's earnings stream.

The lower discount rate applied by the buyer to the earnings stream of the combined firm is a result of the diversification of the riskiness of the earnings that comes from the addition of the new source.

The literature on portfolio theory documents the benefits to be achieved from diversification. While it is recognized that foreign direct investments are not undertaken to obtain a diversified currency portfolio of earnings flows, there is some evidence that the overall risk of a company with worldwide earnings sources is less than that of similar firms with largely domestic income.[7] Nevertheless, the coincidence (albeit imperfect) of primary cyclical trends among major economies of the world may have tended somewhat to reduce the benefits of having a diversified currency portfolio of earnings flows.

Reduction of risk may have been a factor behind acquisitions that were made as part of the follow-the-leader behavior documented in recent research and examined in detail later on.[8] The reduction in risk is derived from the ability of an acquisition to lower the probability that certain extreme variances in earnings may occur. Similarly, acquisitions may have also served as a means of achieving other defensive investment strategies, such as, what has been termed, the exchange of hostage behavior. Acquisitions of this type have occurred in highly oligopolistic industries in which the move of a major market participant, or potential participant, into a position or location

within an industry that is not common to most of the
participants in the industry. Because of the strongly
oligopolistic character of most of the industries in which
multinationals are found, the occurrence of acquisitions,
motivated by the intent to reduce risk, may be expected to
occur with greater frequency during periods when such
defensive investments take place. It is important to note
the difference between the concept discussed above of a
lower discount rate that is derived from a reduction of
risk as perceived by a buyer, and the concept of a lower
discount rate, discussed in the section that follows, which
relates to firms that are growth maximizers (as opposed to
profit maximizers). In that section a lower discount rate
applied by the buyer is systematically used in all investment proposals.

Firms as Growth Maximizers

A second of the three major theoretical foundations for
acquisition behavior involves a shift in focus, from the
point of view of the firm as a profit maximizer to the
view that the firm is a growth maximizer.[9] A number of
authors have structured behavioral models on the basis that
ownership of most corporations is divorced from control.
Under such assumptions, managers may lead firms to maximize
growth rather than profits.[10] Growth maximization results
in part because the rewards of managers are more related to
the size of the firm than to its profitability. Moreover,

the firm is viewed as a bureaucratic organization with no
overall goals, and that whatever objectives the firm may
set for itself will be altered by various interest groups
within the firm that have their own interacting goals.[11]

The impact of the goal of maximizing growth on the
investment polity is that the managers tend to invest more
heavily than profit-maximizers would, with the consequence
that the rate of return on the marginal investments is
below that which the profit maximizer would demand. As the
rate of return on marginal internal investments declines
below the rate of return demanded by the profit maximizer,
the growth maximizer may turn more frequently to acquisitions.[12] The acquisition prospect, particularly if it is a
profit maximizing firm, will most likely apply a higher
discount rate to its earnings flow than will the growth
maximizer.[13]

Thus, to the extent that multinational firms can be
regarded as growth maximizers, they will use a lower discount rate than their smaller, and often owner-managed,
foreign acquisition prospects. It should be noted that,
unlike the lower discount rate concept discussed in the
previous section, it is not necessary for there to be a
reduction in the overall risk of the earnings stream of the
combined firm for an acquisition to take place; the growth
maximizing objective itself is sufficient to generate the

lower discount rate. For this reason, the growth maximizing
theory of acquisitions has been used to explain the occurrence of many of the conglomerate acquisitions that appear
to have no justification in terms of either greater earnings
flows or reduced risk. In particular, the rapid growth of
foreign acquisition activity by multinationals in the late
1960's, especially those few of the conglomerate form
(although not nearly as common in foreign operations as
appears to have been the case within the United States) may
be understandable in terms of the growth maximization
hypothesis.

Divergence in Evaluation

The economic disturbance theory of acquisitions is
often thought of as an alternative explanation to the conglomerate type of acquisitions described above. However,
it also provides insight into possible motives for acquisitions during periods of rapid changes in the economic or
technological environment. The basic premise of the theory
is that during periods of economic or technological
disturbance, past trends become less reliable guides for
developing expectations about the future. As a result,
variations in the valuation of future income streams are
more likely to occur, both because of variations in
estimates of earnings flows and also because of differences
in estimates of levels of risk.[14] Such an increase in the
variance of estimates of future values should generate a

larger number of firms as potential buyers, because
prices will randomly overshoot seller's prices. The
cases in which increases in acquisitions are most likely
to occur would be in industries where concentration
ratios are high (because of the greater difficulty in
valuing future earnings flows where the sum of such flows
are significantly higher than the cost of the firm's
physical assets, as compared to the case of an industry
with low barriers to entry) and in industries where growth
rates are high (because of the greater number of firms that
will be increasing capacity and hence the greater number of
possibilities for valuation discrepancies.) Since these
conclusions have been shown to have apparent validity in
the domestic setting,[15] there is a basis for examining
whether multinationals have shown spurts of acquisition
activity that correspond to periods of technological
innovation within specific industries or to periods of
abrupt economic changes in foreign countries, although the
latter hypothesis would appear to be a bit too all-
encompassing to be at all distinguishable from other
motives.

Other Theories

There are reasons why acquisitions can occur other
than the ones listed. However, in the case of many of
these reasons there is little basis for expecting to find

a systematic influence across the various parent, industry,
or host country characteristics available to this study.
For instance, many acquisitions have no doubt been motivated
by the desire to take advantage of tax-loss carry-forwards
in the company to be acquired, or as a result of the
aggressiveness of promoters. However, for a large statistical
sample study (especially one that does not have financial
data at its command), there is little reason to suspect that
any class of parent firms or industry groups is likely to
be the location of tax-loss carry-forwards or the target of
aggressive promoters.

The Evidence. The first stage of the data analysis
focuses on the influence of the parent firm on acquisition
rates. The question is whether the acquisition theory
suggested in this chapter leads to hypotheses about parent
behavior that are consistent with the evidence. The results
are encouraging.

Industry and host country determinants of acquisition
are examined next to see if the expectations are consistent
with the data. The analysis of the impact of industry
characteristics on acquisition rates brings to bear substantial supportive material from the literature of the
economics of industrial organization.

The final chapters focus on the use of acquisitions
during the periods of defensive investment behavior. Here

again the role of acquisitions borne out by the evidence is
consistent with the model discussed in this section.

FOOTNOTES TO CHAPTER IV

1
J. W. Markham, "Survey of the Evidence and Findings on Mergers,"
in Business Concentration and Price Policy (Princeton: National
Bureau of Economic Research, 1955); R. L. Nelson, Merger
Movements in American Industry, 1895-1956 (Princeton: Princeton
University Press for the National Bureau of Economic Research,
1959).

2
Celler-Kefauver Act: Sixteen Years of Enforcement, Antitrust
Subcommittee, Committee on the Judiciary (Washington, D.C.:
1967); Current Trends in Merger Activity, 1968 Statistical
Report, Bureau of Economics, Federal Trade Commission, March
1969.

3
M. Gort, "An Economic Disturbance Theory of Mergers,"
Quarterly Journal of Economics, November 1969, p. 636.

4
Ibid.

5
R. Vernon, "Organization as a Scale Factor in the Growth of
Firms," in J. W. Markham and G. F. Papanek, eds., Industrial
Organization and Economic Development (Houghton Mifflin
Company, 1970).

6
Robert Z. Aliber, "A Theory of Direct Foreign Investment,"
in C. P. Kindleberger (ed.), The International Corporation
(Cambridge, Mass.: The M.I.T. Press, 1970; also see Robert
Z. Aliber, "The Multinational Enterprise in a Multiple
Currency World," in John H. Dunning (ed.), The Multinational
Enterprise, Praeger Publishers, 1971, p. 53.

7
A. M. Rugman, "Foreign Operations and the Risk of Profits,"
unpublished paper, 1974, cited in H. G. Baumann, "The
Determinants of the Pattern of Foreign Direct Investment:
Some Hypotheses Reconsidered."

8
F. T. Knickerbocker, Oligopolistic Reaction and Multinational
Enterprise (Boston: Division of Research, Harvard Business
School, 1973).

9
In particular, see, R. L. Marris, The Theory of "Managerial"
Capitalism (Glencoe, Ill.,: Free Press, 1964).

10
    W. J. Baumol, Business Behavior, Value and Growth (New
York: MacMillan, 1959); J. K. Galbraith, The New Industrial
State (Boston: Houghton Mifflin, 1967); E. T. Penrose,
The Theory of Growth of the Firm (Oxford: Oxford University
Press, 1959); O. Williamson, The Economics of Discentionary
Behavior: Managerial Objectives in a Theory of the Firm
(Englewood Cliffs: Prentice-Hall, 1964).

11
    For example, R. J. Monsen, Jr. and A. Downs, "A Theory of
Large Managerial Firms," Journal of Political Economy,
June 1965, pp. 221-236; R. M. Cyert and J. G. March,
A Behavioral Theory of the Firm (Englewood Cliffs: Prentice-
Hall, 1963); F. Machlup, "Theories of the Firm: Marginalist,
Behavioral, and Managerial, "American Economic Review,
March 1967, pp. 1-33.

12
    J. McGowan, "The Effect of Alternative Antimerger Policies
on the Size Distribution of Firms," Yale Economic Essays, V
(Fall 1965).

13
    R. L. Marris, "Galbraith, Solow and the Truth About
Corporations," The Public Interest, Spring 1968, p. 44.

14
    Cellar-Kefauver Act, op. cit., p. 37.

V. Parent Size and Foreign Acquisitions

Despite the fact that the overall trend of foreign acquisitions by U.S. multinationals continued to rise well into the late 1960's, there was considerable variation in the acquisition activity among individual firms. Some firms consistently acquired more heavily than others. Nearly one-fourth of the 187 firms examined had average acquisition rates over time above 70% as contrasted to another quarter of the sample that acquired less than 25% of their foreign subsidiaries. Moreover, contrary to the rapidly increasing interest in acquisitions over time exhibited by the total sample, the trend among the individual firms was one of generally less reliance on acquisitions (at least in comparison to the sample as a whole) as time passed. This somewhat paradoxical phenomenon--what might be described as a falling trend for each participant within a rising trend for the universe of firms--appeared to be comprehensible when the effect of parent size on acquisition rates was singled out.

Parent Size and Risk Aversion

Parent size was not an unlikely choice for an explanatory factor of the variation in foreign acquisition rates among firms. After all, parent size has been a useful barometer for other characteristics of the foreign investment process.

For instance, firm size has been shown to correlate strongly with the level of foreign direct investment.[1]

Firm size also appears to have had a significant
influence on foreign acquisition activity. Firm size has,
among its many effects, an important influence on the
perceived level of risk in making a foreign investment.
A large firm is likely to have a broad portfolio of returns
and risks in its overall operations. Any one investment
is likely to be relatively small in relation to the total
assets of the firm. Particularly if the firm has subsidiaries
in many different countries (and currencies), the perceived
effect of potential variance in the future total income
stream due to a single investment may not appear to have as
high a level of risk to a large firm as may be the case for
the small firm. The potential variance in the income stream
of a foreign investment may have a substantially greater
effect on the overall income pattern of a small firm, especially
if the foreign investment is large compared to the parent.

In the process of investing overseas, therefore, the
small firm is likely to place a higher value on reducing
risk than the large firm. It is the ability to reduce the
perceived level of risk that is the key to why acquisitions
ought to appear more attractive to the small firm as a
vehicle for investing overseas; and hence the important
effect that parent size is expected to have on the rate of
acquisition observed among the foreign subsidiaries of U.S.
multinational firms.

This is not to claim that variations in parent size
alone "explains" the patterns observed in foreign acquisitions.

Ind-ed, as subsequent analysis will show, other factors,
whose variations appear to be largely independent of the
variation in parent size, also have a systematic influence
on acquisition rates: namely, the extent of parent diversification, the degree of entry concentration by industry,
the level of product differentiation by industry, as well
as other selected industry and host country characteristics.
Nevertheless, the persistent effect of parent size on acquisition rates appears to dominate other influences.

The Evidence

The data gives good support to the expected relationship between parent size and foreign acquisition activity.
The largest firms show a significantly lower rate of
acquisition among foreign manufacturing subsidiaries than
do the smaller firms, as shown in Table 5-1. However, as
this data includes all subsidiaries ever formed, it does
not tell whether the same relationship was valid over
recent periods of time.

Further analysis indicated that the pattern also held
over various periods of time and for different locations. As
shown in Table 5-2, small parent firms tended to make greater
use of acquisitions than larger firms both in developed
economies as well as in the LDC's, and consistently over the
pre-World War II and postwar periods. In this test, parent
firms were divided into two groups and subsidiaries were
assigned to the time period in which they began manufacturing.

Table 5-1

Percentage of Acquisitions Among Foreign Manufacturing
Subsidiaries Classified by Size of Parent
(As Measured by Sales in 1970)

Value of Sales of Subsidiary's Parent in 1970	Percentage of Acquisition
$100 - 399 million	50.
$400 - 599 million	53.
$600 - 999 million	53.
$1 - 2 billion	50.
Over $2 billion	38.

Source: J.W. Vaupel and J.P. Curhan, The World's
Multinational Enterprises (Boston: Harvard Business
School, 1973), p. 358.

Table 5-2

Percentage of Acquisitions Among Foreign Manufacturing
Subsidiaries Defined by the Size of the Parent Firm*

Level of Sales of Parent	Percentage of Acquisitions for the Period in which Subsidiary Began Manufacturing		
	Pre-1946	1946-1957	1958-1967
Total Foreign Subsidiaries Outside U.S. & Canada			
Low Sales Parents	27.	35.	50.
High Sales Parents	27.	31.	45.
Subsidiaries Located in Europe Only			
Low Sales Parents	33.	46.	56.
High Sales Parents	32.	33.	54.
Subsidiaries Located in LDC's Only			
Low Sales Parents	26.	25.	47.
High Sales Parents	20.	28.	34.

*
Parent size is based on the level of sales in 1966; firms
classified as having "high" sales parents were those with
sales greater than the median of parent sales; while "low"
sales firms were those with sales less than or equal to
the median.

Note: When no source is listed, the data is drawn from the Multinational
Enterprise Data Base, and more often than not cross-checked for
consistency with statistics listed in James W. Vaupel and Joan P.
Curhan, The Making of the Multinational Enterprise (Boston: Harvard
Business School, 1973).

Firm Size and Location. The greater risk of foreign
investment to the small sized firm may cause these
firms to select locations that help reduce various aspects
of risk. The large firm gains from the diversification of
risk over many subsidiaries as well as facing less risk in
terms of the absolute size required for a foreign investment. Proximity to the United States (e.g., Canada or
Mexico) would involve more familiar areas and less risk to
the acquiring firm. Also, countries with similar language
or customs (e.g., United Kingdom) would also help reduce
risk. It is likely, therefore, that smaller firms might
have a greater tendency than larger firms to seek locations
that might help reduce the riskiness of foreign investment
(such as Mexico, Canada, and the U.K.). A simple calculation of the percentage of acquisitions and the relative
number of new subsidiaries formed in these countries by
both large and small firms confirms this notion. Smaller
firms (as classified by parent firms with low level of
parent sales) consistently tended to invest more heavily in
Canada, Mexico and the United Kingdom (as measured by subsidiaries formed in each country as a percentage of total
foreign subsidiaries) than did the larger firms, as shown
in Table 5-3 . The smaller firms also showed a slightly
higher level of acquisitions in these countries during

Table 5-3

Effect of Parent Size (as Measured by Level of Parent Sales in
1966) and Selected Location on Percentage of Acquisitions
and Number of Subsidiaries Formed

	Period in Which Subsidiary Began Manufacturing					
Location and Level of Parent Sales	Percentage of Acquisitions Among Subsidiaries Formed			Subsidiaries Formed in Each Country as a Percentage of Total Foreign Subsidiaries		
	Pre-1946	1946-1957	1958-1967	Pre-1946	1946-1957	1958-1967
Subsidiaries Located in Canada Only						
Low-Sales Parents	31.	51.	79.	27.	21.	11.
High-Sales Parents	39.	57.	69.	26.	19.	10.
Subsidiaries Located in Mexico Only						
Low-Sales Parents	17.	30.	59.	3.	11.	8.
High-Sales Parents	21.	39.	51.	5.	8.	7.
Subsidiaries Located in U.K. Only						
Low-Sales Parents	37.	48.	72.	20.	12.	9.
High-Sales Parents	37.	32.	63.	14.	9.	8.
All Foreign Subsidiaries Outside U.S.						
Low-Sales Parents	27.	35.	50.	100.	100.	100.
High-Sales Parents	27.	31.	45.	100.	100.	100.

the 1958-1967 period, althouth the pattern was slightly
irregular during the earlier periods. While this evidence
is hardly enough to establish the point conclusively, it
confirms the expected direction of the hypothesis.

Foreign Experience. Long experience in foreign
operations would also tend to reduce the risk of new investment. The seasoned investor views the world with less
uncertainty than the newcomer firm. The length of foreign
experience clearly is likely to be highly correlated in
most cases with the measure of the size of the parent or
with the measure of the size of the firm in specific foreign
industries. Nevertheless, as there can be important differences between parent firm size and the length of foreign
experience, it is worth exploring the correlation between
acquisition activity and various measures of the length of
foreign experience of the parent firm.

The knowledge of dealing in foreign environments that
is acquired through years of operation is an important asset
to the experienced firm, regardless of the size of the parent.
After a firm has compiled a sizeable record of foreign experience, the uncertainties of operating in foreign environments may be correspondingly reduced. The marginal cost of
reducing the uncertainty of operating in foreign environments decreases with experience. Thus, the ability of an
acquisition to reduce uncertainty might not be as effective,
for the particular reasons cited above, to a firm with

greater foreign experience. Moreover, the experienced
firm would have built up an asset in the knowledge of how
to set up a new plant from scratch and this asset could be
used in foreign markets at little marginal cost, thus
reducing both the effective cost and the corresponding
uncertainty of a start-up operation. With less perceived
risk of variation in possible outcomes from a (possibly
lower-cost) formation of a new subsidiary, more experienced
firms might tend less to use acquisitions as a means of
entry or as a way of achieving defensive investments.
Rather than pay to obtain knowledge directly or to face a
higher level of risk than bearable, the small firm is
likely to turn to a foreign takeover.

A clear pattern emerges from the evidence. Lesser
experience in foreign operations implies greater reliance
on acquisitions. While the data in general tend to confirm
the expected tendency, tests have the limitations. A
direct causal relationship between the foreign experience
of the parent and acquisition activity is difficult to
prove. Because of the expected positive correlation between
the level of the parent's foreign experience and other
parent characteristics (e.g., firm size) and industry
characteristics, the true partial effects of foreign
experience are not easily isolated.

Nevertheless, all of the measures of foreign
experience of the parent serve well as proxy measures for
the "size of the parent firm" in the special context of
using the "size of the parent firm in foreign markets" as
a measure of "parent size." Parent size in this context
relates not to the size of the parent firm worldwide, but
more specifically to the size of the parent operations
outside the United States.

Various measures of foreign experience were examined:
(1) The date of the first foreign manufacturing plant;
(2) the number of years of foreign manufacturing experience
(very similar to the first measure); (3) the number of
foreign manufacturing subsidiaries; and (4) the geographic
diversity of foreign manufacturing. All foreign subsidiaries were classified into groups according to the level
of parent foreign experience at the time the subsidiary
entered the parent system. For instance, for the third
measure, subsidiaries were grouped according to whether
they were among the first to third subsidiaries in the parent
system, the fourth to tenth, and so on. The percentage of
acquisitions for each group of subsidiaries was calculated.

Parent firms that first began foreign manufacturing
prior to 1920 sought acquisitions at consistently lower
rates than parent firms that began foreign manufacturing
in later periods, as shown in Table 5-4. Similarly for firms
first manufacturing in foreign markets during the interwar

Table 5-4

Percentage of Acquisitions Among Manufacturing Subsidiaries
Classified According to the Period in Which the Parent First
Established a Foreign Manufacturing Subsidiary)

Location and Period in which Parent First Established a Manufacturing Subsidiary Abroad	Period in which Subsidiary Began Manufacturing		
	Pre-1946	1946-1957	1958-1967
Total Foreign Subsidiaries Outside U.S. & Canada			
Pre-1920	22.	30.	41.
1920-1945	35.	30.	47.
1946-1967	*	43.	54.
Subsidiaries Located in Europe Only			
Pre-1920	25.	31.	50.
1920-1945	45.	34.	55.
1946-1967	*	55.	59.
Subsidiaries Located in LDC's Only			
Pre-1920	18.	27.	29.
1920-1945	24.	29.	37.
1946-1967	*	24.	51.

*
Not applicable since, by definition, parent firms moving overseas
after 1946 did not establish a   foreign subsidiary prior to 1946.

period (1920-1945). Parent firms that had the least foreign
experience--those that first established foreign manufacturing subsidiaries during the period of 1946 to 1967--
showed very high acquisition rates for their new subsidiaries. This was particularly apparent in Europe, where
these newcomers to the foreign scene acquired over 55% of
all new subsidiaries during their first few years of foreign
manufacturing experience--from 1946 to 1957. Acquisition
rates for the more experienced firms over the same period
of time was significantly lower--30 to 35%.

Inexperienced firms also showed a higher tendency to
acquire overseas, when experience was measured by the number
of years of foreign manufacturing activity. Subsidiaries
formed during the early years of a firm's foreign manufacturing experience were acquired with greater frequency than
subsidiaries formed in later years. This negative relationship,shown in Table 5-5, between subsidiary acquisition rate
and number of years of parent foreign manufacturing
experience was particularly evident in the postwar years,
not only in Europe but even more so in the less developed
countries. The least experienced firms showed a dramatic
increase in their use of acquisitions over the postwar
period. Firms with foreign experience of 10 years or less
acquired nearly three-fifths of their subsidiaries during
the period 1958-1967, compared to a rate of 40% for such
firms in the previous decade. Even more notable was the

Table   5-5

Percentage of Acquisition Among Manufacturing Subsidiaries
Classified According to the Length of Time Since the
Parent Firm Began Foreign Manufacturing

Location and Number of Years of Parent Foreign Manufacturing Experience When Subsidiary Entered Parent System	Period in which Subsidiary Began Manufacturing		
	Pre-1946	1946-57	1958-67
Total Foreign Subsidiaries Outside U.S. & Canada			
< 11 years	32 .	39 .	59 .
11-20 years	23 .	35 .	45 .
21-40 years	27 .	31 .	49 .
> 40 years	25 .	28 .	41 .
Subsidiaries Located in Europe Only			
< 11 years	36 .	50 .	64 .
11-20 years	31 .	38 .	48 .
21-40 years	30 .	36 .	55 .
> 40 years	27 .	30 .	51 .
Subsidiaries Located in LDC's Only			
< 11 years	24	23	56
11-20 years	19	34	43
21-40 years	24	27	39
> 40 years	27	23	32

record for acquisitions by newcomers in the less developed
countries. The rate of acquisitions for these least
experienced firms more than doubled over the period 1958-
1967 compared to the record of similar firms in the previous ten years. The record for the most experienced firms
also showed increased rates of acquisition but not of the
same magnitude.

The higher rate of acquisitions observed among the
early foreign subsidiaries in a parent system, compared to
the acquisition rate among later subsidiaries, gave further
confirmation to the link between foreign experience and
acquisitions. Subsidiaries among the first ten to enter a
parent system were generally acquired more frequently than
subsidiaries that were among the 25th and beyond, as shown
in Table 5-6. Exceptions to this pattern were uncovered
in the 1958-1967 period. While the expected relationships
were particularly strong in the LDC's over this period, the
reverse was the case in Europe. This was in sharp contrast
to the early postwar period where the early subsidiaries
were acquired at much higher rates than later subsidiaries.
Closer examination of the data showed the dimensions of the
extraordinarily heavy volume of new investment in the EEC
during the period 1958-1967, following the formation of
the EEC, which may have had an important effect in altering
the pattern of acquisitions for large firms. During the

Table 5-6

Percentage of Acquisitions Among Manufacturing Subsidiaries
Classified According to the Order of Subsidiary Entry
into the Parent System

Location and Rank of Manufacturing Subsidiaries by Order of Entry Into Parent System	Period in which Subsidiary Began Manufacturing		
	Pre-1946	1946-57	1958-67
Total Foreign Subsidiaries Outside U.S. & Canada			
1st-3rd subsidiaries	29.	37.	46.
4th-10th	32.	30.	45.
11th-25th	19.	35.	48.
> 25th	22.	26.	48.
Subsidiaries Located in Europe Only			
1st-3rd	33.	51.	50.
4th-10th	35.	35.	49.
11th-25th	27.	39.	55.
> 25th	31.	30.	56.
Subsidiaries Located in LDC's Only			
1st-3rd	19.	23.	50.
4th-10th	31.	24.	43.
11th-25th	15.	31.	41.
> 25th	07.	24.	37.

1958-1967 decade, the number of subsidiaries formed in the
EEC was double the number formed in all the years previous
to 1958. Moreover, most of these subsidiaries (more than
80%) were formed by parent firms that already had more than
10 foreign subsidiaries prior to 1958. In fact by 1958,
very few firms were still yet to make their first few
foreign forays; only 12 of the 187 firms waited until after
1958 to establish their first foreign manufacturing subsidiary. Thus, there were not many examples of firms investing
in their first few subsidiaries in the EEC after 1958. The
small sample size for the 10th or under subsidiary category
in Table 5-6 may have caused some random bias. More
important however, was the flood of activity in the EEC
among the larger firms--those with 11 or more subsidiaries.
That many firms took advantage of the formation of the EEC
to increase rapidly their number of foreign investments was
alluded to above. The shift to acquisitions as a method of
entry was common to all sized firms. In fact, of the 143
firms in the sample that had investments in the EEC, close
to 60% made their first acquisition in the EEC after 1958.
The number of acquisitions made in the EEC in the decade
1958-1967 was three times the number of acquisitions made
in all the years prior to 1958. Thus, large firms, which
in previous periods had appeared to have had less need than
small firms to turn to acquisitions, responded to the formation of the EEC with a shift to takeovers. Underlying the

shift was most likely a desire to act quickly to be able to
match the moves of their competitors into the EEC. Evidence
of the increased use of acquisitions as a means of making
defensive investments is examined in greater detail in the
last part of this study.

Geographic Diversity. Wide geographic spread, like
other dimensions of foreign experience, operated to reduce
foreign acquisition activity. Firms with operations in few
countries showed greater reliance on acquisitions for their
new investments. As Table 5-7 shows, firms with smaller
geographic spread acquired more frequently than firms with
greater geographic spread.

In summary, tests using the various measures of foreign
experience (as proxys for parent size in foreign operations)
support the hypothesis that acquisition rates among subsidiaries are likely to be negatively correlated with foreign
experience (size in foreign operations). It is also worth
noting that measures taken from the "stock" of foreign
subsidiaries (such as geographic diversity) and measures
taken from the "flow" of foreign subsidiaries (such as the
sequential order of entry of subsidiaries) led to similar
conclusions about the effect of foreign experience on
acquisition rates.

Table 5-7

Percentage of Acquisitions Among Manufacturing Subsidiaries
Classified According to the Geographic   Diversity of the Parent*

Location and Level of Geographic Diversity of Parent in 1966	Period in which Subsidiary Began Manufacturing		
	Pre-1946	1946-1957	1958-1967
Total Foreign Subsidiaries Outside U.S. and Canada			
High Geographic Diversity	26.	30.	46.
Low Geographic Diversity	32.	39.	49.
Subsidiaries Located in Europe Only			
High Geographic Diversity	31.	35.	54.
Low Geographic Diversity	37.	43.	55..
Subsidiaries Located in LDC's Only			
High Geographic Diversity	20.	26.	37.
Low Geographic Diversity	26.	30.	44.

---

*Geographic diversity is based on the number of countries in which
the parent had foreign manufacturing subsidiaries in 1966, with
firms with more than 13 subsidiaries being classified as having
"high" geographic diversity.

Is Country Bias Possible? Among the possible alternative explanations of the observed relationship between
parent size and frequency of acquisitions is that country
bias might account for the lower acquisition rate for
larger firms. Presume that larger firms, having exhausted
investment opportunities in the developed world, were
forced to turn more frequently over time to the LDC's for
investments. As acquisition rates among subsidiaries formed
in LDC's are lower than for subsidiaries in developed countries (for example, see Table 5-7) the larger firms would
gradually show an overall lower acquisition rate than their
smaller competitors as a result of the country distribution
of their activities.

The data give no support for this hypothesis. In the
first place, the breakdown of acquisition rates by parent
size and country grouping shown earlier in Table 5-2,
revealed that smaller parents maintained higher acquisition
rates even in the developed countries of Europe. Moreover,
smaller firms have increased the investments in LDC's as a
proportion of their total investments at a slightly higher
rate than have larger firms, as shown in Table 5-8 . In
fact, the total number of acquisitions made by small firms
during the 1958-1967 period was actually greater than that
made by large firms, as contrasted to the period prior to
1946 when the number of acquisitions in LDC's made by small

Table 5-8

Subsidiaries Formed in LDC's as a Percentage of
Total Subsidiaries Formed Outside the
United States and Canada Classified
by Size of Parent Firm

Location and Size of Parent	Period Subsidiary Began Manufacturing		
	Pre-1946	1946-1957	1958-1967
Subsidiaries Located in LDC's			
Low Sales Parents	22.	48.	39.
High Sales Parents	36.	49.	37.
Subsidiaries Located in Latin America Only			
Low Sales Parents	22.	42.	30.
High Sales Parents	30.	42.	26.
Subsidiaries Located in LDC's of Asia and Africa Only			
Low Sales Parents	0.*	6.	9.
High Sales Parents	6.	7.	11.

*
less than   5 percent.

firms was less than half the number made by large firms.
Thus, the notion that country bias may explain part of the
effect of parent size on acquisition rates is not supported
by the data.

Summary of the Effects of Parent Size on Foreign Acquisition Rates

By all measures, increasing parent size tends to reduce
the need for foreign acquisitions. The consistency with which
this pattern is observed gives credence to the underlying model
that acquisitions are used in large measure as a risk minimizing
tool. The declining trend in acquisition rates among large and
experienced foreign investors is a rather surprising observation
when put in the context of an overall rising trend in the rate
of foreign acquisitions. This merely emphasizes the dependence
that small firms have placed on acquisitions and highlights the
fact that foreign expansion by small and relatively inexperienced
firms was particularly heavy during the post war period.

Looking beyond the horizon of parent size the effects on
foreign acquisition rates of a number of other factors can be
brought into focus. Strong presumptions exist in the literature
of economic theory regarding the impact that strategies of product
differentiation have on the use of acquisitions--a subject that
will be taken up next. Beyond this, selected industry characteristics are also expected to help explain some of the observed
variance in industry acquisition rates in accordance with the
model of acquisition used so far. Also not to be neglected are
acquisition patterns induced by the characteristics of the
host country.

FOOTNOTES TO CHAPTER V

[1]
Firm size has been shown to be statistically related to
direct investment, by many, in particular, T. Horst, "Firm
and Industry Determinants of the Decision to Invest Abroad:
An Empirical Study," Review of Economics and Statistics,
August 1972, pp. 258-266.

VI.   Diversification Through Foreign Acquisition

Diversification has generally not been regarded as a major motivation for U.S. investments abroad.[1] Horizontal or vertical strategies have been attributed to most foreign ventures.[2] Moreover, few conglomerates have actively extended their acquisitive tendencies abroad.

Nevertheless, evidence exists of firms with significant levels of foreign diversification. Many firms with strategies of foreign product differentiation (and subsequent organizational adaptation) have been discussed by Stopford and Wells.[3] Moreover, in 1966 close to 25% of major U.S. multinationals were classified by Stopford as having high levels of foreign product diversity, as shown in Table 6-1 . In addition, of all foreign subsidiaries formed prior to 1968, 30% were established by U.S. parents with considerable foreign product diversity--i.e., producing in 10 or more foreign industries in 1968. By contrast, only 13% of all foreign subsidiaries formed prior to 1968 were established by U.S. parents with narrow foreign product lines--i.e., producing in three or fewer foreign industries in 1968, as shown in Table 6-2 . By all estimates foreign product diversity was more than a minor phenomenon.

Table 6-1

Domestic Product Diversity Versus Foreign
Product Diversity of Parent Firms in 1966

Domestic Product Diversity*	Number of Parent Firms Classified by Foreign Product Diversity*				
	None	Low	High	Total	Percent of Total
None	26	0	0	26	14.
Low	28	37	0	65	40.
High	71	3	31	71	44.
Total	57	68	37	162	100.
Percent of Total	35.	42.	23.	100.	

*
"None"indicates that a firm has all its products in a
single two-digit SIC industry; "low" indicates that a
firm has products in more than one industry, but that
one product line is of dominating importance; "high"
indicates that a firm has products in many industries,
and no dominant product line.

Source: John M. Stopford and Louis T. Wells, Jr.,
Managing The Multinational Enterprise (New York: Basic
Books, 1972), p. 35.

Table   6-2

Percentage Breakdown of Number of Foreign Manufacturing
Subsidiaries When Foreign Product Diversity of Parent
is Classified by U.S. Product Diversity of Parent

U.S. Product Diversity of Parent (Number of U.S. Industries of Subsidiary's Parent System)	Foreign Product Diversity of Parent (Number of Foreign Industries in Subsidiary's Parent System)				Total Percent	Total Number of Subsidiaries
	1-3	4-9	10-19	>20		
1-3	45.	55.	0.	0.	100.	388
4-9	15.	61.	17.	8.	100.	1447
10-19	10.	71.	14.	5.	100.	1460
>20	1.	30.	52.	17.	100.	862
All Subsidiaries	13.	57.	22.	8.	100.	
Total Number of Subsidiaries	544	2393	901	333		4162

Role of Acquisitions in Foreign Diversification.
The relationship between diversification and acquisitions
has not been thoroughly explored in an overseas setting,
although evidence has been presented of a strong
correlation between the two in the U.S. market. [4] However,
it would appear that acquisitions have played an important
role in foreign diversification of U.S. multinationals.
An examination of foreign subsidiaries formed outside the
primary 3-digit SIC of the parent system indicated the
importance of acquisitions to diversification. Over 53%
of these diversifying subsidiaries were acquired compared
to a 45% rate of acquisition among subsidiaries formed in
the same 3-digit SIC as the parent, as shown in Table 6-3.
Classified on this basis, foreign diversification comprised
60% of all subsidiaries, leaving only 40% for horizontal
expansion overseas. Diversifying acquisitions were close
to double the number of acquisitions in the same 3-digit
SIC of the parent, as shown in Table 6-4, a slightly
different breakdown of the same information in Table 6-3.

Foreign Diversification: An Extension of Domestic
Diversification. Some clues as to the role of acquisitions
may be revealed from the relationships of foreign diversification to domestic diversification. Many aspects of foreign

Table   6-3

Foreign Diversification Versus Horizontal Expansion Overseas

(Percentage Breakdown of Foreign Manufacturing Subsidiaries
by Relationship of Primary Industry of Subsidiary to Primary
Industry of Parent Firm Classified by Method of Entry)

Primary 3-digit SIC Industry of Subsidiary	Acquisi- tion	Forma- tion	Other	Total Parent	Total No. of Subsi- diaries
Outside 3-digit SIC of Parent Firm	53.	45.	2.	100.	2868
In Same 3-digit SIC of Parent Firm	45.	53.	₋2.	100.	1892
Total Subsidiaries	50.	48.	2.	100.	4760

Table 6-4

Foreign Diversification Versus Horizontal Expansion Overseas

(Percentage Breakdown of Foreign Manufacturing Subsidiaries
by Method of Entry Classified by Relationship of Primary
Industry of Subsidiary to Primary Industry of Parent Firm)

Primary 3-digit SIC Industry of Subsidiary	Acquisi- tion	Forma- tion	Other	Total Subsidiaries
Outside 3-digit SIC of Parent Firm	64 .	56 .	64 .	60 .
In Same 3-digit SIC of Parent Firm	36 .	44 .	36 .	40 .
Total Percent	100 .	100 .	100 .	100 .
Total Number of Subsidiaries	2373	2296	91	4760

diversification appear as an extension of a diversification
process already under way in U.S.-operations, except with
a lag. That domestic diversification should begin first is
logical. As noted by Caves, firms with skills that are
deployable outside a firm's main line of business ought
first seek to be employed in domestic diversification.[5]
Moreover, the product life cycle model similarly
holds that products are first innovated to serve domestic
markets before they are taken overseas. Serving foreign
markets typically first takes place via the export route.
As foreign markets mature, openings for domestic U.S.
products develop and pressures for local production increase.

Operating in parallel to the flow of products overseas
are changes in the organizational structure of large firms.
Stopford and Wells developed a taxonomy of organizational
growth which showed how the build-up of expertise for
handling diverse markets and products first occurred in
the United States before being implanted to perform
similarly in foreign settings.[6] The ability to cope with
domestic diversity preceeded the evolution of a similar
capacity overseas.

Another natural reason for a lag in foreign product
diversity is the large number of products exported to
foreign markets undertaken by U.S. multinationals. These
exports were not recorded as additions to foreign products

and thus do not count in the foreign product diversity measure.

That foreign product diversity lags, but follows closely behind, domestic product diversity was first noted in Table 6-1 . According to Stopford and Wells' classification, 42% of U.S. multinationals had a higher level of U.S. product diversity than foreign product diversity; and in no instance was the reverse true.[7] However, for the other 58% of the firms, foreign diversity was on a par with the domestic side.

Looking at the same phenomenon from a slightly finer angle yielded the same conclusions. This time product diversity was represented by the number of industries in which the parent manufactured. Table 6-5 classified each subsidiary according to the relationship between domestic and foreign product diversity of the parent firm. Domestic and foreign product diversity of the parent firms were equal for roughly one-third of all subsidiaries. Domestic diversity was clearly higher than foreign diversity for 50% of the subsidiaries. Foreign diversity was higher in only 15% of the cases, although in cases of the most extreme diversity in foreign operations (i.e., firms with foreign manufacturing in greater than 20 3-digit SIC industries) parents of 56% of the subsidiaries had greater

Table 6-5

Percentage Breakdown of Number of Foreign Manufacturing
Subsidiaries when U.S. Product Diversity of Parent is
Classified by Foreign Product Diversity of Parent

U.S. Product Diversity of Parent (Number of U.S. Industries in Subsidiary's Parent System)	Foreign Product Diversity of Parent (Number of Foreign Industries in Subsidiary's Parent System)					
	1-3	4-9	10-19	>20	All Subsidiaries	Total Number of Subsidiaries
1-3	32.	9.	0.	0.	9.	388
4-9	40.	37.	27.	35.	35.	1447
10-19	27.	43.	23.	21.	35.	1460
>20	1.	11.	50.	44.	21.	862
Total Percent	100.	100.	100.	100.	100.	
Total Number of Subsidiaries	544	2393	901	333		4162

foreign diversity than domestic product diversity, as
shown in Table 6-5.

Why Use Acquisitions in Foreign Diversification? The
link between foreign diversification and acquisition has
been suggested by various characteristics of acquisitions
discussed earlier in the study: the ability to provide for
a reduction in risk, complementarity of resources, and
potentially rapid growth.

Risk confronting the new entrant to a previously
untouched foreign industry is likely to be high. Even if
prospective returns are also potentially large, the risk-
reduction is important to the diversifying firm that has
little experience in the industry to draw upon. For a
subsequent expansion within the same industry, the level of
risk is not likely to be so great, and the value of acquisitions less. Evidence from U.S. setting indicates that
diversification (which, although not necessarily achieved
through acquisition, most likely involved a significant
amount of acquisition activity) has contributed to a
reduction of overall level of riskiness of diversifying
firms, as indicated by lower variance in earnings flows
of diversified firms.[8]

Moreover, the diversifying parent may be seeking
foreign outlets to utilize its set of skills beyond its
existing set of industries. Opportunities for

complementarity between resources of the parent and the
acquired firm may be high. This set of skills, be it a
core of technical, marketing or management skills that
have been developed at a substantial sunk cost, may be
transferable with relatively low marginal cost to new
applications. The prospective acquisition with complementary abilities which in combination with the parent's
skills could generate returns beyond levels possible by
these same firms separately. Gort's research on the
domestic setting indicates that firms from less profitable
and slow growing industries tend to be more active
diversifiers.[9] These firms face limited potential for
utilizing valuable skills within the confines of sluggish
industry settings.

It is also likely that highly diversified firms have
developed greater agility in adding new product lines
within their organizational structures than narrow product
line firms. This might contribute to a higher ratio of
success in absorbing acquisitions into the parent. These
firms have been shown to have been able to withstand
pressures arising from other external sources, such as
dealing with outside joint venture partners within their
systems.[10] Such organizational flexibility would appear
to improve the chances that acquisitions of new product
lines could be undertaken with some degree of success.

The carryover of domestic acquisition activities into
the foreign sphere is also likely to tie in naturally with
foreign diversification. Already noted earlier in this
study has been the close parallel between cycles of acquisition activity in the domestic and foreign markets. In
addition, there are numerous instances in which a parent
firm acquires another domestic firm that happens to have a
set of foreign subsidiaries. A not insignificant number of
foreign subsidiaries of the 187 firms in the Multinational
Enterprise Data Base were established in this manner.
Furthermore, antitrust restrictions in the United States may
stimulate diversifying acquisitions domestically, which
eventually may spill over into the foreign sphere.

Evidence. Foreign diversification has already been
shown to have exhibited heavier dependence on acquisitions
than horizontal expansion overseas (Table 6-3). A further
breakdown of diversification over various time periods
gives further support to the relationship. First, looking
at diversity as measured by the product diversity of a
parent's domestic operations, higher product diversity is
consistently associated with higher acquisition rates,
although with little significant differences in acquisition
rates over the last decade of observation, as shown in
Table 6-6.

Table 6-6

Percentage of Acquisitions and Parent's Product Diversity in the United States*

Product Diversity in the U.S.	Percentage of Acquisitions for the Period in which Subsidiary Began Manufacturing		
	Pre 1946	1946-1957	1958-1967
Total Foreign Subsidiaries Outside U.S. & Canada			
Low Diversity	22.	30.	46.
High Diversity	32.	35.	48.
Subsidiaries Located in Europe Only			
Low Diversity	29.	37.	54.
High Diversity	35.	39.	55.
Subsidiaries Located in LDC's Only			
Low Diversity	14.	24.	39.
High Diversity	28.	30.	40.

*Product diversity in the United States was classified as "high" if the parent system manufactured in 10 or more 3-digit SIC industries in the United States.

However, when the level of foreign product diversity
was used as a measure of diversification, the preference by
highly diversified firms for acquisitions was more significant as shown in Table 6-7 . Foreign product diversity
would appear to be more logical than domestic product
diversity as an indicator of the level of acquisition rates
because domestic diversification tends to proceed faster
than foreign diversification. Thus, a high measure for
domestic product diversity might well overstate the degree
of product diversity in the foreign sphere where firms had
not yet undertaken a program of foreign diversification.
In such cases, foreign acquisition rates would be reflecting
the level of foreign diversification rather than the higher
level of domestic product diversification.

Growth Rates, Acquisitions and Diversification.
Diversification through acquisition has often been associated
with the goal   of rapid growth. A couple of items tend
to confirm this on the foreign side. First the firms with
high product diversity have more subsidiaries than firms
of low product diversity. Particularly if foreign product
diversity is used as the measure of product diversity, the
average number of subsidiaries per highly diverse firm is
35, almost double the number for less diverse firms, as
shown in Table 6-8 . Moreover, growth in terms of numbers
of subsidiaries was also significantly higher among the

Table 6-7

Percentage of Acquisitions and the Parent's Product
Diversity Abroad*

Product Diversity Abroad	Percentage of Acquisitions for the Period in Which Subsidiaries Began Manufacturing		
	Pre 1946	1946-1957	1958-1967
Total Foreign Subsidiaries Outside U.S. & Canada			
Low Diversity Abroad	23.	29.	43.
High Diversity Abroad	30.	35.	50.
Subsidiaries Located in Europe Only			
Low Diversity Abroad	29.	37.	50.
High Diversity Abroad	34.	39.	57.
Subsidiaries Located in LDC's Only			
Low Diversity Abroad	17.	19.	37.
High Diversity Abroad	24.	32.	41.

*Product diversity abroad was classified as "high" if the parent
system manufactured in 5 or more different 3-digit SIC industries
in foreign countries in 1966.

Table   6-8

Number of Foreign Manufacturing Subsidiaries
Per Firm Classified According to the Level
of Parent Product Diversity

Level of Parent U.S. Product Diversity*	Number of Subsidiaries Formed pre-1968	Number of Parents	Number of Subsidiaries Per Firm
Low Diversity	2350	94	25.
High Diversity	2829	93	30.
Level of Parent Foreign Product Diversity*			
Low Diversity	1766	89	20.
High Diversity	3413	98	35.

*
 Product diversity in the United States was classified as
"high" if the parent system manufactured in 10 or more
different 3-digit SIC industries in the United States in
1966. Product diversity abroad was classified as "high"
if the parent system manufactured in 5 or more different
3-digit SIC industries in foreign countries in 1966.

highly diversified firms'. Firms with highly diverse
foreign activity almost tripled the number of their foreign
subsidiaries over the period 1957-1968. By contrast, growth
of firms with lower foreign product diversity,while not
quite so rapid, more than doubled their size over the same
period.

The link between growth rates and acquisitions is
revealed by dividing parent firms into high growth and low
growth groups. High growth firms show higher acquisition
rates, but not convincingly so, as shown in Table 6-9 .
The problem here is that the measure of growth used here
is based on domestic not foreign sales.

The evidence for the 1958-1967 period confirm the
direction of the hypothesis. For years earlier than 1950,
the growth rates of parent firms may have been significantly
different--thus the data is not really relevant to the
hypothesis.

Diversification and Success with Acquisitions. Related
to the strategy of product diversification has been the issue
of developing planning procedures and organizational structures
to cope with diversity. The success or lack of success at
integrating diversifying acquisitions into the parent system
has been the subject of a number of research efforts.[11] For
example, diversifying acquisitions have been shown by Kitching
to be significantly more risky than horizontal acquisitions.[12]

Table 6-9

Percentage of Acquisitions and the Growth of the Parent
Firm (as Measured by the Growth of Parent Sales
During Period 1950-1966)

Level of Growth in Sales of Parent	Percentage of Acquisitions for the Period in which Subsidiary Began Manufacturing		
	Pre 1946	1946-1957	1958-1967
Total Foreign Subsidiaries			
Low Growth Parents	33.	38.	46.
High Growth Parents	29.	35.	55.
Subsidiaries Located in Europe Only			
Low Growth Parents	34.	37.	52.
High Growth Parents	37.	38.	59.
Subsidiaries Located in LDC's Only			
Low Growth Parents	24.	27.	34.
High Growth Parents	21.	26.	45.

Another yardstick of the success of acquisitions within the multinational organizations is the rate of exit of acquisitions from the parent system. While there was no separate breakdown for diversifying acquisitions, the data from the multinational firm study indicated that acquisitions had slightly higher exit rates from the parent system than did subsidiaries formed de novo, as shown in Table 6-10. If the confiscated and expropriated subsidiaries are excluded from the calculation, the acquired subsidiaries exit at a rate 1.5 times the exit rate for newly formed subsidiaries. These results would simply confirm the notion that the chances of success are slighly higher for newly formed subsidiaries than for acquired subsidiaries.

These results raise the issue that in certain respects acquisitions are slightly more risky than newly formed subsidiaries. This point has not been missed in the popular literature on acquisitions. Nevertheless, the magnitude of additional risk inherent in an exit rate for acquisitions if less than 10% higher than the corresponding exit rate for newly formed subsidiaries would appear acceptable in light of the offsetting advantages. Moreover, if it were true that acquisitions were selected for investments that had higher average levels of risk than de novo investments, a higher exit rate for acquisition would appear natural.

Summary of the Effects of Diversification on Foreign Acquisition Rates

The significant degree of diversification found in the foreign operations of U.S. multinationals appears to have been

Table 6-10

Percentage Breakdown of Manufacturing Subsidiaries
by Subsidiary's Method of Exit From Parent
System Classified According to
Subsidiary's Method of
Entry Into Parent
System

Subsidiary's Method of Exit from Parent System

Subsidiary's Method of Entry Into Parent's System[1]	Sold	Confiscated or Expropriated	Liquidated, Function Ended	Liquidated, Function[2] Continued	Did Not Exit
Newly formed	3.6	1.5	3.5	5.2	86.2
Reorganized	7.1	1.2	1.2	8.2	82.3
Acquired	4.0	0.5	4.4	11.0	80.1

[1]A subsidiary is considered to have exited when parent ownership is less than 5%.

[2]"Function continued" indicates that the functions of exiting subsidiary were continued by subsidiaries elsewhere in the parent system.

accomplished to a large extent through the vehicle of
acquisitions. Acquisitions serve the diversifying firm
not only by reducing the risk of investment in product
lines that are "new" to the foreign sphere, but also by
providing a medium through which the parent can quickly
allow the foreign operation to have access to key parent
skills. That foreign diversification appears to lag domestic
diversification, not only in timing but also in degree, is
consistent with the underlying product life cycle model of
U.S. foreign investment, i.e., products innovated for the
U.S. markets subsequently find foreign outlets.

Beyond the effects of parent size and diversification
on foreign acquisition rates industry structure and conduct
have independent influences of their own. The next two
chapters examine respectively the theoretical foundation
and the evidence for such influence.

FOOTNOTES TO CHAPTER VI

1
R. E. Caves, "International Corporations: The Industrial
Economics of Foreign Investment," Economia, February 1971,
p. 3.

2
E. R. Barlow and I. T. Wender, Foreign Investment and
Taxation (Englewood Cliffs, N.J.: Prentice-Hall, 1955),
p. 159.

3
J. M. Stopford and L. T. Wells, Jr., Managing the Multinational Enterprise (New York: Basic Books, 1972).

4
Federal Trade Commission, Economic Report on Mergers
(Washington: Government Printing Office, 1968), p. 48.

5
Caves, "Industrial Economics," op. cit.

6
Stopford and Wells, Managing the Multinational, op. cit.

7
Ibid.

8
Richard J. Arnold, Diversification and Profitability Among
Large Food Processing Firms, U.S. Department of Agriculture
Economic Report No. 171 (Washington: Government Printing
Office, 1971).

9
M. Gort, Diversification and Integration in American Industry
(Princeton: Princeton University Press, 1962).

10
Stopford and Wells, Managing the Multinational, op. cit.

11
For general commentary, see Acquisitions in Europe,
Business International, 1973. Studies of the ingredients of
success were taken up by John Kitching, "Why Do Mergers
Miscarry," Harvard Business Review, November-December 1967,
and in "Winning and Losing with European Acquisitions,"
Harvard Business Review, March-April 1974.

12
Kitching, Acquisitions in Europe, p. 62.

VII. Market Structure and Acquisition Theory

Market structure is likely to influence foreign
acquisition rates in ways independent of the effects of
parent characteristics just discussed. Industry variations in market conduct both in the United States and
abroad have been in part explained by the influence of
market structure. The effect of market structure on the
particular aspect of conduct of interest here--acquisi-
tion behavior of multinationals --is expected to shed
some light on the industry variations in foreign acquisition rates. Evidence from the literature of industrial
organization is used in combination with acquisition theory
to develop some basic notions about the effect of industry
structure on foreign acquisitions. Examination is focussed
on the impact of economies of scale (production as well as
other functional areas), product differentiation, concentration, and market stability.

Economies of Scale: Production. The possibility of
achieving efficiency improvement through greater economies
of scale in production is often cited as an important
reason for acquisitions. It would appear, however, that
conventional logic overstates the case. The likelihood
of increasing technical economies of scale would be
greatest in horizontal acquisitions, but purely horizontal

foreign acquisitions--those narrowly defined as being in
the same 3-digit SIC industry as the primary 3-digit SIC
as the parent--comprised only one-third of total foreign
manufacturing acquisitions (Table 6-3 in Chapter VI).
Moreover, there are limitations to the amount of increase
in technical efficiency (or as sometimes referred to,
functional "synergy") that can be expected even from
horizontal acquisitions. Many acquisitions are made by
multi-plant firms with location-specific production;
this is likely to be as true for foreign acquisitions,
where multi-plant operations are common. This factor
severely limits the ability of the acquiring firm to
increase production economies of scale. The literature
points out the fact that many large firms are multi-product
and multi-plant operations with often larger than optimal
scale. Stigler has argued that optimal scale is typically
smaller than is commonly found to exist in larger firms in
the United States.[1]   Studies by Pratten and Dean in the
United Kingdom similarly indicated that for many industries,
production economies can be reached at levels that do not
comprise a significant percentage of national output.[2]

Alberts also argues that many firms reach levels of
costs minimization even in industries with conditions far
from perfect competition.[3] Studies in Canada by Reuber

and Roseman[4] and in the United States by Gort[5] found
little or no significance in economies of scale as an
explanatory variable for industry rates of acquisition.
This also implies that small sized firms might not
necessarily suffer a great disadvantage in production
economies relative to larger competitors. In sum,
weight of evidence would lead to the conclusion that
economies of scale in production are not expected to be
a significant factor motivating foreign acquisitions.

Economies of Scale: Marketing and Other Functional
Areas. There has been an increasing body of evidence to
show that economies of scale in other functional areas may
be significant. Acquisitions may have greater ability
to increase economies of scale in these functional areas.
Complementarity of resources may also contribute to an
advantage due to economies of scale in cases where an
acquisition provides excess resources to a functional area
in the acquiring firm that was operating at below efficient
scale.

The area of marketing is a good example. Bain indicated
that economies of scale in marketing in some industries
would justify larger-sized firms and greater degrees of
concentration than would production economies,[6] especially
in industries where marketing costs comprise at least 50%

of the cost to the final consumer. Although Simon and
others have disagreed with this proposition,[7] Mueller
argues that the explanation for growing concentration in
consumer goods manufacturing is the advantage of large
scale in promotion and distribution.[8] The potential
benefits from economies of scale in the marketing area
would constitute the basis for expecting a positive correlation between the rate of acquisition and a suitable
measure of marketing intensity. (Further to this point are
similar arguments made in the following section on product
differentiation.)

Economies of scale have been suggested in other
functional areas. In the area of finance, often cited as
an advantage possessed by large firms, a study by Merrett,
Howe, and Newbould[9] indicates evidence of economies of scale
in raising capital. Aliber argues further that ability to
finance in the United States capital market creates a cost
advantage to the U.S. multinational firm compared to firms
forced to borrow in foreign capital markets, where the
higher interest rates (as the case may be) more than offset
the risk of currency depreciation.[10] Higher capitalization
rates that would be expected for U.S. firms would provide
a natural advantage for foreign acquisitions.

Research and Development (R&D) is another area where
economies of scale may play a role. The literature shows
that, although there is evidence of economies of scale in
R&D, there is little to indicate that firms of large size
have higher rates of technological innovation. Scherer
concluded in his study of U.S. firms that "the evidence
does not support the hypothesis that corporate bigness is
especially favorable to high inventive output."[11] Nor does
industry concentration necessarily lead to higher rates of
technological progress, as noted by Stigler[12] and
Markham.[13] Williamson extends this point elsewhere to conclude that, even though mergers between two small or
medium-sized firms rarely have negative effects on technical
productivity, the case for positive effects for mergers
between large firms was much less clear.[14] Further,
studies by Peck[15] in the United Kingdom and Caves[16] in the
United States conclude that there is little support for
mergers or monopoly as a way to promote R&D expenditure.
This is evidenced by the fact that concentration is lower,
on average, in certain groups of industries that are
characterized by relatively good performance and which at
the same time possess relatively simple and static
technology, such as the food, textiles, and furniture
industries.

Furthermore, the bulk of R&D activity for U.S. multinationals has been maintained in the United States.[17]
Skill at technical innovation has been a major source of
advantage for U.S. firms to spread overseas. As such,
concentration of R&D activities within the United States
would minimize the desire to acquire overseas to achieve
higher economies of scale in the R&D effort. Thus it does
not seem likely that foreign acquisitions have been
motivated by a desire to achieve economies of scale in
the R&D area.

Finally, a case can be made for the likelihood of
economies of scale in the use of skilled manpower, i.e.,
in the organizational capabilities of large firms. In ways
somewhat similar to the lumpiness that is a characteristic
of large capital investments, high risk and large scale
are important elements in the decision to expand a firm's
human capital.[18] This would apply to human capital investment in a number of functional areas, in particular
marketing, but perhaps general management and R&D as well.
The potential advantages to existing firms for achieving
economies of scale in these areas, relative to the problems
facing a new entrant, appear to be significant, although the
magnitude of such advantage has not been quantitatively
determined. These advantages may be even more significant

to multi-plant firms where functional activities can be
spread over higher levels of output and result in a lower
unit cost for that overhead. Caves found that such multi-
plant economies were a significant determinant of inter-
industry variation in the level of foreign investment in
Canada (although this did not hold for the United Kingdom).[19]
McManus and others have similarly argued that multi-plant
economies constitute an important cost advantage to the
firm producing across national boundaries.[20]   Recent work
by Scherer indicates that the extent of multi-plant operations
within a country is closely linked to the size of the market
served in relation to the minimum optimal plant size.[21]
However, Scherer found no statistically significant relationship between recent merger activity and the extent of multi-
plant operations. Nevertheless, as multinational firms span
across many countries, it would appear that centralized
skills could be spread out over larger numbers of plants
than would be possible for local competitors. In sum, the
possibility of generating multi-plant economies in central
skills could provide a logic for firms to expand across
national boundaries through acquisition.

No broad conclusion about the effect of economies of
scale on foreign acquisitions can be made without reference
to particular functional areas. The likelihood of achieving
significant benefits in production scale economies through
cross border acquisitions appears small. A similar case can
be made for R&D skills. On the other hand, the marketing
area might be a logical candidate for generating scale
economies via the acquisition route. Selecting variables
to serve as proxies for these hypothesized relationships
is a problem to be taken up in the next chapter.

Product Differentiation. Foreign acquisitions may also
have an important role to play in industries marked by
high levels of product differentiation. Industries characterized by product differentiation might stimulate higher
rates of acquisitions for basically two reasons: the potential
for acquisitions to generate additional returns from underutilized resources, and the ability of acquisitions to
reduce the risk of surmounting the high barriers to entry
(or expansion) within differentiated industries.

Industries characterized by product differentiation may
have significant potential to increase returns to underutilized marketing resources. That such industries have
played such an active role in direct investment overseas

may in part be attributable to the existence of such
resources. Caves cited this as "the basis for direct
investment: the successful firm producing a differentiated
product controls knowledge about serving the market that
can be transferred to other national markets at little or
no cost."[22] The ready transferral of human capital assets
from the parent to foreign markets is accomplished easily
via the acquisition route. Underutilized domestic resources
can be combined with complementary sets of accessible local
skills (in production or distribution). Although the
transfer of skills can be directed through new investment
by the parent, an acquisition has the advantage of reducing
the risk (particularly important in the cases of new
entrants) and speeding up the generation of returns.

     Entry into a product differentiated industry entails
substantial risk because of the size of the absolute
barrier to entry. Absolute cost barriers to entry involve
shifts in the average cost curve itself, rather than
movements along the average cost curve as is the case for
the economies of scale barriers discussed in the previous
section. Bain concluded that entry barriers are more
frequently attributed to product differentiation than to
economies of scale in production.[23] In product differentiated
industries not only are entry barriers high, but expansion

within the industry is risky. As noted by Buzzell and Nourse, innovation costs and commercial risks involved in launching new products are substantial, giving a distinct advantage to firms of large size.[24] The ability to reduce the high risks involved in expanding or establishing a foothold within differentiated industries would thus appear to be an incentive for the use of foreign acquisitions particularly to a small firm or even to a large firm with only a "small" position in such an industry.

To focus exclusively on the marketing function as a determinant of product differentiation would overlook the influence of R&D. Research intensity might well be an alternate indicator of the industry level of product differentiation. R&D expenditures that are directed largely to new products and product development may contribute heavily to product differentiation, although there may be a significant lag between the timing of R&D outlays and the subsequent creation of tangible products or useful knowledge.

However, selecting an appropriate measure is left to the next chapter. For current purposes, it is well to conclude that the need for large size and sufficient scale to maintain competitiveness in product differentiated industries suggests that foreign acquisitions may play an active role in the growth of such industries.

Concentration. On the relationship between industry concentration and industry rates of acquisition, various arguments were suggested in the discussion of acquisition theory and its implications for the multinational firm. In general, the theories of acquisition would expect acquisition frequency to be positively related to industry concentration: in particular, the monopoly power theory and economic disturbance theory.

The monopoly power theory of acquisitions argues that the benefits of obtaining increased market power would be greater in highly concentrated industries than in industries with low levels of concentration. Acquiring into a concentrated industry would forestall an increase overall productive capacity. It would not put additional downward pressure on profitability as would be the case if a new capacity were created. Furthermore, in industries with low concentration there is less capability for increasing market power through acquisitions.

The economic disturbance theory of acquisitions also argues for a positive relationship between industry concentration and the rate of acquisitions. The basis for the argument is that there is likely to be a greater divergence during unstable periods in prices set by buyers and sellers in highly concentrated industries than in less concentrated

industries. This results from the fact that economic disturbances are likely to cause greater difficulty for
evaluating acquisition prospects in highly concentrated
industries than in less concentrated industries. The
primary reason for a lower level of difficulty in assessing
acquisition prospects in less concentrated industries is
because valuation of these firms is presumed to be closer
to the cost of the firms' assets than would be the case in
highly concentrated industries. Greater divergence in
prices of buyers and sellers would lead to a higher
incidence of acquisitions.[25]

A higher rate of acquisition in concentrated industries
could also be expected in industries where factor inputs are
so tightly controlled that entry would be feasible only
through the acquisition of existing inputs. Such cases
would place a prohibitive cost to assembling the factors
from scratch. Although this argument is more related to
certain types of absolute cost barriers to entry, such
barriers are more likely to exist in highly concentrated
industries. These specific highly concentrated industries
may expect to have higher rates of acquisition for new
entrants.

Evidence confirming a general positive relationship
between industry concentration and acquisition rates was

found by Gort in his investigation of merger trends in the
United States. A strong positive correlation was found
between the merger rate and the levels of industry concentration for data gathered in the 1950's.[26]

Concentration and Acquisition Rates in Target Industries:
A Negative Correlation. The arguments above suggest that
acquisition rates ought to be higher in highly concentrated
industries. Despite these strong arguments, it is also possible
to suggest reasons why a negative relationship might be found
between the level of industry concentration and industry rates
of acquisition.

Part of the conflict revolves around whether the level
of concentration of the industry being examined refers to the
industry which is the target for the acquisition or to the
industry of the firm doing the acquiring. The distinction
between target and source industries is important when selecting
a measure for the level of concentration. Since the evidence
in this study examines the level of concentration and acquisition rate of the industry of the subsidiary, i.e., the target
industry, a number of the arguments for a positive correlation
between concentration and rate of acquisition are put aside
because they are based on the relationship between the level
of concentration and rates of acquisition of the parent firm,
i.e., the source industry.

For horizontal investments, both target and source are
the same. However, in the case of diversification, the target
industry is likely to have characteristics quite different from
the source industry, as has been shown by Gort and others.[27]

High concentration in the source industry may cause firms to
seek to diversify elsewhere. If acquisitions play an active
role in diversification, there would be a positive correlation
between concentration of the investing firm's industry and the
acquisition rate among new subsidiaries. At the same time,
however, the target industry attracting new investment will also
show a rising acquisition rate. As target industries are
likely to be less concentrated than the source industry, the
correlation between industry concentration and acquisition rate
may be negative, especially if industries with low concentration
are good targets for diversification. Gort's analysis of
diversification,[28] as well as Horst's recent work,[29] would
suggest that target industries are somewhat attractive because
barriers are lower at the time of entry than would be expected
later as the industry matures.

Additional factors might be expected to lead to a negative
correlation between industry concentration and industry rates of
acquisition. The question of the availability of acquisition
prospects (discussed in greater detail in the section on host
country characteristics) may have an important influence on
acquisition activity. Industries with low levels of concentration
can be expected to have a larger number of prospects available
to meet the criterion desired by the potential acquiring firms.
In more concentrated industries, lack of availability of
acquisition prospects could lead to lower acquisition rates.

Another factor that might have a negative effect on the
relationship between concentration and acquisitions is the
relative size of acquisitions. In a data base constructed

largely in terms of numbers of subsidiaries, industries with
large numbers of small acquisitions would appear out of proportion to industries with small numbers of large acquisitions.
Highly concentrated industries are likely to show a smaller
number of acquisitions occurring than in less concentrated
industries. Using the rate of acquisition as a measure of
acquisition activity may reduce potential distortion of this
kind. Nevertheless, it is likely that less concentrated industries will have a flow of small acquisitions taking place to
a higher degree than in highly concentrated industries. This
effect could contribute to a negative relationship between
acquisition rates and concentration levels.

To summarize the arguments concerning the effect of
concentration on acquisition rates, it would appear that part
of the conflict can be resolved if the effect of concentration
on acquisition rates in target industries is separated from
the effect on acquisition rates of concentration in the parent
industry. Concentration in the target industry would appear
to lean in the direction of having a negative effect on
acquisition rates, while the opposite may be said of the
effect of concentration in the parent industry.

Industry Stability: The Flow of New Entrants. Regardless of market structure, the entry of a newcomer into an
industry is expected to have an important impact on market
behavior. In the case of a new foreign firm entering a
domestic market, the new entrant is likely to produce more
active rivalry within the industry than would be the case
if a similar entry was made by a local firm.[30] The
foreign entrant is likely to introduce new tactics of
competition and be less likely to abide by the whatever
rules of the game were in effect previously. The result
might be a greater amount of competitiveness beyond the
normal joint maximization pattern of oligopolistic inter-
dependence. The generation of uncertainties and disturbances
in the market might lead to a slightly more active use of
acquisitions to reduce the risks of expansion, either by
other new entrants or by existing participants.

In the process of U.S. direct investment overseas, the
flow of new U.S. entrants to the foreign scene may have
added to the instability in market behavior. Knickerbocker
found that the greater the percentage of U.S. parent firms

that were established abroad in a given industry prior to
1946, the less need there was for follow-the-leader behavior
in the post-war era.[31]   It would seem likely that instability
of this kind would be positively related to the degree of
foreign acquisitions undertaken to avoid just such risks.

Industry Stability and Economic Disturbance. Industry
variation in acquisition rates may also be related to the
occurrence of periods of industry instability. In addition
to industry instability that may arise from inflows of new
entrants (discussed above), a variety of other economic
shocks may affect acquisition rates. Gort's findings give
support to the hypothesis that rapid change in technology
or wide movements in security prices may induce greater
variance in valuations among buyers and sellers of firms,
resulting in higher acquisition rates.[32]   Systematic
occurrence of higher rates of economic disturbance in
specific industries may be difficult to pinpoint. However,
industries characterized by rapid changes in technology
that lead to new product or process innovations would appear
to fit this pattern. Gort found a high level of correlation
(.74) between merger rates and his proxy variable for
technological change (a ratio of technical personnel to total
employment per industry).[33]

A correlation between technological change and acquisition rates would also be expected for firms investing overseas. U.S. multinational firms have been characterized by
comparatively high levels of technological innovation. Thus
the link between innovation and acquisition rates may be
expected to carry over into foreign markets as well.

Summary of Expected Industry-Related Influences on Foreign
Acquisition Rates

Industry characterístics are expected to have separate
dimensions of influence on acquisition rates, largely independent of the effects of parent characteristics. From among
the factors expected to have significance for acquisition
rates, a number have been deleted. Economies of scale in
production process appear unlikely as a motivation for foreign
acquisitions. In the R&D area, while scale economies might
be attractions for domestic acquisitions, little effect is
expected on the foreign side of operations. Scale in the
raising of capital would be more a function of parent size
than industry factors. Marketing and other human intensive
skills would be areas where scale economies might be enhanced
through foreign acquisitions. In particular, the occurrence
of mulgi-plant operations might act to spur the rate of
foreign acquisition based on scale considerations. Attraction
to foreign acquisitions would appear to be high in product
differentiated industries. While this industry characteristic
overlaps slightly with the economies of scale in marketing,

the propensity for risk reduction in product differentiated industries gives additional motivation for foreign acquisitions.

Industry concentration would appear to pull in both directions. The more plausible direction is that the foreign industries into which parent firms invest are likely to be attractive for acquisitions where concentration levels are low. Finally, industry instability would also be expected to be stimulant for foreign acquisitions. Two particular forms of instability are likely to have this effect: a rapid inflow of new parent firms into an industry and the frequent occurrence of economic or technological disturbances to industry trends.

Definition of variables to test these hypotheses along with the examination of the relevant evidence follows.

FOOTNOTES TO CHAPTER VII

1
G. J. Stigler, "The Case Against Big Business," in
E. Mansfield, Monopoly Power and Economic Performance
(Norton, 1964).

2
C. Pratten and R. M. Dean, "The Economies of Large-Scale
Production in British Industry," Occasional Papers, No. 3.
Cambridge University Press, 1970.

3
W. W. Alberts, "Profitability and Growth by Merger," in
W. W. Alberts and J. E. Segall (eds.), The Corporate
Merger (Chicago, 1966), p. 255.

4
G. L. Reuber and F. Roseman, The Take-Over of Canadian
Firms 1945-1961: An Empirical Analysis, Special Study
No. 10, Economic Council (Ottawa: Queen's Printer, 1969).

5
M. Gort, "An Economic Disturbance Theory of Mergers,"
The Quarterly Journal of Economics, November 1969, p. 632.

6
J. S. Bain, Barriers to New Competition (Cambridge, Ma-s.:
Harvard University Press, 1956).

7
J. L. Simon, "Are There Economies of Scale in Advertising,"
Journal of Advertising Research, Vol. 5, June 1968.

8
W. F. Mueller, "The Celler-Kefauver Act: 16 Years of
Enforcement," (Washington, D.C.: U.S. Government Printing
Office, 1967).

9
A. J. Merrett, M. Howe, and G. Newbould, Equity Issue and
the London Capital Market (London: Longmans, 1967),
Chapter 8.

10
R. Z. Aliber, "The Multinational Enterprise in a Multiple
Currency World," in J. H. Dunning, ed., The Multinational
Enterprise (New York: Praeger Publishers, 1971), pp. 49-56.
See also "A Theory of Direct Investment," in C. P.
Kindleberger, ed., The International Corporation (Cambridge:
The M.I.T. Press, 1970), pp. 17-34.

11
  F. M. Scherer, "Firm Size, Market Structure, Opportunity and the Output of Patented Inventions," American Economic Review, Vol. LV, December 1965.

12
  G. J. Stigler, "Industrial Organization and Economic Progress," in L. D. White (ed.), The State of Social Sciences, Chicago, 1956, p. 278.

13
  J. W. Markham, "Market Structure, Business Conduct, and Innovation," American Economic Review, May 1965, p. 326.

14
  O. E. Williamson, "Economics as an Antitrust Defense: The Welfare Trade-offs," American Economic Review, Vol. LVIII, March 1969, p. 29. Also, "Innovation and Market Structure," Journal of Political Economy, February 1965.

15
  M. J. Peck, "Science and Technology," Britain's Economic Prospects, in R. E. Caves and Associates (eds.), (London: Allen & Unwin, 1968).

16
  Ibid., p. 299.

17
  Raymond Vernon, Sovereignty at Bay (New York: Basic Books, 1971), p. 136.

18
  Raymond Vernon, "Organization as a Scale Factor in the Growth of Firms," in J. W. Markham and G. F. Papanek (eds.), Industrial Organization and Economic Development (Boston: Houghton-Mifflin, 1970).

19
  R. E. Caves, "Causes of Direct Investment: Foreign Firms' Share in Canadian and United Kingdom Manufacturing Industries," Review of Economics and Statistics, February 1975, p. 292.

20
  J. C. McManus, "The Theory of the Multinational Firm," in G. Paquet (ed.), The Multinational Firm and The Nation States (Don Mills, Canada: Collier-MacMillan, 1972), pp. 66-93. Also, H. C. Eastman and S. Stykolt, The Tariff and Competition in Canada (Toronto: MacMillan, 1967).

21
F. M. Scherer, "The Developments of Multi-plant Operation in Six Nations and Twelve Industries," Kyklos, no. 1, 00.124-139.

22
R. E. Caves, "International Corporation: The Industrial Economics of Foreign Investment," Economica, February 1971, p. 6.

23
J. S. Bain, Barriers to New Competition, op. cit., p. 142.

24
R. D. Buzzell and R. E. Nourse, Product Innovation and Food Processing, 1954-1964 (Boston: Division of Research, Harvard Business School, 1967).

25
M. Gort, "An Economic Disturbance Theory of Mergers," Quarterly Journal of Economics, November 1969.

26
Ibid., p. 635.

27
Ibid., p. 637.

28
Ibid.

29
T. Horst, At Home Abroad: A Study of The Domestic and Foreign Operations of the American Food-Processing Industry (Cambridge: Ballinger, 1974).

30
R. E. Caves, "Industrial Economics," op. cit., p. 15.

31
F. T. Knickerbocker, Oligopolistic Reaction and Multi-national Enterprise (Boston: Harvard Business School, 1973), pp. 87-95.

32
M. Gort, op. cit.

33
Ibid., p. 635.

VIII. Market Structure and Acquisitions: The Evidence

How the rate of foreign acquisitions by U.S. multinationals was expected to have been influenced by various
industry characteristics was detailed in the previous
chapter. The focus here is on the pragmatic: selecting
relevant variables and interpreting the results of the tests.

The Data and Limitations

Three primary sets of data were used in testing the
hypotheses, the first two of which were subsets of the main
data base for foreign subsidiaries. The first subset of
data was a 3-digit SIC sample for 22 industries. It contained only a limited number of industry variables. The
second subset of data was a 2-digit SIC sample for 12 industries which had a larger coverage of industry characteristics.
The third set of data consisted of the data base on parent
firms from the Multinational Enterprise Study. It contained
information on 184 parent firms (information on 3 of the 187
firms was not on the parent data base). Despite the fact
that industry characteristics were the subject of the current
analysis, selected parent characteristics were used as proxies
for industry characteristics when relevant to the analysis.
In particular, for parent characteristics that were relatively
independent of parent size and at the same time directly
associated with the industry variables being examined, the
impact correlation of these parent characteristics with
foreign acquisition rates were of related interest. Where

industry variables were strongly correlated with parent size,
an examination of parent size and the variable in question
could better reveal where parent size may be the driving force
behind the direction of the relationship.

Interpretation of the results was cautious for many
of the tests. The primary problem for certain tests was
lack of foreign industry data. Many tests related to U.S.
industry characteristics; where foreign industry data was
required, U.S. data was in general used as a proxy. For
example, foreign concentration levels were assumed to bear
similarity to U.S. levels. As noted in the previous chapter,
tests of certain industry characteristics were omitted from
this section precisely for the reason that there was a lack
of foreign data and there was a low probability that U.S.
data would serve instead.

Correlation Among Important Variables

Before discussing the evidence relating industry characteristics to acquisition rates, it is important to indicate
the level of correlation that exists between the industry
variables themselves. As shown in Table 8-1, the correlation
between selected industry characteristics was fairly low,
with certain exceptions, for the 22 industry 3-digit SIC
sample. Similarly, an indication of the degree of correlation
among various parent characteristics, particularly those
referred to in the analysis to follow, was also rather low,
as shown in Table 8-2. Of note is the low level of correlation
of parent size with a number of important variables.

Table 8.-1

Simple Correlation Matrix for Variables Used
in 3-Digit SIC Industry Analysis

(22 3-Digit SIC Industries)

	C4	VA	NP	CP	P46
ECI	.01	-.46	.12	-.21	-.35
C4		.54	.05	-.19	-.01
VA			-.15	-.12	.30
NP				-.12	.36
CP					-.23

Abbreviation	Variable Name
ECI	Entry Concentration Index
C4	Four-firm Concentration Ratio, Adjusted
VA	Value-added per Plant (plants with 20 employees or more)
NP	Number of Plants (with 20 employees or more)
CP	Consumer-Producer Dummy Variable (consumer industries = 0, producer industries = 1)
P46	Percentage of U.S. Parents Establishing Foreign Manufacturing Facility Prior to 1946

Table 8-2

Simple Correlation Matrix for Variables Used
in Parent Data Base

(184 U.S. Parent Firms)

	R&D	ADV	#CO	A/P	CONC
S	- .08	- .10	.32	.51	.13
R&D		.19	.09	.03	- .08
ADV			.13	- .06	- .12
#CO				.22	.11
A/P					.00

Abbreviation	Variable Name
S	Sales in 1963
R&D	Ratio of R&D expenditures to sales in 1966
ADV	Ratio of advertising expenditures to sales in 1966
#CO	Number of foreign countries with manufacturing plants in 1963
A/P	Assets per plant in 1964

The Evidence Relating to the Major Hypotheses

Following the order presented in the previous chapter, evidence on the effect of major industry characteristics on acquisition rates is now examined.

Economies of Scale: Production. The expectation that potential for economies of scale in production would not show up as a significant motivation for foreign acquisitions was confirmed. As a rough measure of technical economies of scale, value-added per plant was used. The value-added per plant measure was taken from 1963 Bureau of Census Figures.[1] Total value-added per 3-digit SIC industry was divided by the number of establishments in the same industry with 20 or more employees. As shown in Table 8-3 the strongly negative cor5elation (-.55) found between value-added per plant and the rate of foreign acquisitions appears to indicate that economies of scale are acting as a significant depressant acquisitions.

The results are consistent with observations of the effect of the level of physical capital intensity (as measured by the ratio of assets/sales) of the parent firm on foreign acquisition rates. As can be seen from Table 8-4, physical capital intensity demonstrated a negative relationship with acquisition rates consistently over recent time periods. It is worth noting that value-added per plant was highly correlated (.83) with the capital intensity measure. The explanation for the significant negative effects that these two variables have on acquisition rates probably reflects the

117.

Table 8-3

Correlation Coefficients of Selected Industry Characteristics
with Percentage of Acquisition by Industry

(22 3-digit SIC Industries)

Industry Characteristic	Coefficient of Correlation with Percentage of Acquisitions
Eight-firm concentration ratio, adjusted	-.12
Four-firm concentration ratio, adjusted	-.05
Marginal eight-firm concentration ratio, adjusted	-.30
Eight-firm concentration ratio	-.44
Four-firm concentration ratio	-.39
Marginal eight-firm concentration ratio	-.34
Value added per plant	-.55
Number of plants	+.52
Percentage of Parent Firms Manufacturing in Foreign Markets pre-1946	-.21
Consumer-Producer Products (consumer= 0, producer=1)	-.32

Table 8-4

Percentage of Acquisitions and Physical Capital Intensity
of Parent*

Level of Parent Physical Capital Intensity	Percentage of Acquisitions During Period in which Subsidiary Began Manufacturing		
	Pre-1946	1946-1957	1958-1967
Total Foreign Subsidiaries Outside U.S. & Canada			
Low Capital Intensity	26.	35.	52.
High Capital Intensity	28.	30.	43.
Subsidiaries Located in Europe Only			
Low Capital Intensity	32.	42.	58.
High Capital Intensity	33.	34.	51.
Subsidiaries Located in LDC's Only			
Low Capital Intensity	22.	26.	44.
High Capital Intensity	21.	28.	36.

*Physical Capital Intensity is defined as the ratio of assets to
sales in 1966.

partial effects of parent size, since both variables show
modest positive correlations with parent sales. This would
be consistent with earlier conclusions that acquisition rates
are negatively related to parent size.

Multiplant Firms. A test of the hypothesis that the
occurrence of multiplant firms might lead to higher acquisition
rates was not specifically tested. However, the highly positive correlation, +.52, (see Table 8-3) between the rate of
acquisition and the number of plants per industry (with 20
or more employees) might constitute indirect evidence in support
for this hypothesis. A more direct test would be to use a
variable based on the percentage of shipments in the United
States made by multiplant firms, as was used by Caves. In a
more general sense, the positive correlation may suggest that
availability of acquisition prospects is an important factor
in determining the rate of acquisitions in target induustries.
This factor will be raised in the discussion of the negative
correlation between concentration ratios and the percentage of
acquisitions.

Economies of Scale: Other Functional Areas. The only
functional area that was expected to show a likely chance of
generating economies of scale was the marketing function. In
the R&D area, for instance, there was little support for the
notion that economies of scale in foreign R&D activities was
an objective of any systematic nature among multinationals.
As far as the marketing function is concerned, there is a
major problem in measuring scale economies in marketing that

would be distinguishable from a measure of product differentiation. As such, tests using the marketing intensity
variable were felt to represent better the product differentiation hypothesis; so no test was made of the economies of
scale hypothesis in the marketing area.

Product Differentiation. The evidence gave strong
confirmation to the hypothesis that high levels of product
differentiation tend to increase acquisition rates. All
three samples showed systematic positive correlations. At
the 2-digit SIC industry level there was a positive correlation
of .47 between the rate of acquisition at the 2-digit level and
the ratio of advertising to sales. The advertising to sales
ratio was aggregated to the 2-digit level from data obtained
from News Front in March 1966.

At the 3-digit SIC level, an indirect test was set to
distinguish between consumer goods industries (dummy variable
set = 0) and producer goods industries (dummy variable set = 1).
A negative correlation of -.32 between the dummy variable and
acquisition rates at the 2-digit SIC level indicates a higher
rate of acquisition for the consumer-oriented industries than
for producer goods industries. This is based on the assumption
that consumer goods industries are more advertising intensive
than producer goods industries.

Finally, the parent sample also indicated a strong
positive relation between acquisition rates and advertising
intensity, as shown in Table 8-5. This is a strong piece of
evidence, particularly in light of the fact that parent size

Table 8-5

Percentage of Acquisitions and the Advertising Intensity of
the Parent*

Level of Parent Advertising Intensity	Percentage of Acquisitions During Period in which Subsidiary Began Manufacturing		
	Pre-1946	1946-1957	1958-1967
Total Foreign Subsidiaries Outside U.S. & Canada			
Low Advertising Intensity	24.	.29.	39.
High Advertising Intensity	29.	34.	53.
Subsidiaries Located in Europe Only			
Low Advertising Intensity	28.	32.	47.
High Advertising Intensity	43.	42.	59.
Subsidiaries Located in LDC's Only			
Low Advertising Intensity	20.	20.	28.
High Advertising Intensity	20.	31.	47.

*Advertising Intensity is defined as the ratio of advertising to sales in 1966.

is not highly correlated, -.10, (see Table 8-2) with the
level of advertising intensity.

It should also be noted that the research intensity
of a given industry might also serve as an indicator of the
level of product differentiation of the industry. This would
be particularly true of R&D expenditures were spent largely
on new products or on product developments and as such would
contribute to the product differentiation, which in many
fundamental ways is similar to the expected differentiating
effects of advertising expenditures. However, there is an
important limitation. There is often a significant lag between
the timing of expenditures on R&D and the subsequent creation
of new products or new knowledge transferrable to foreign
markets. A correction would have to be made for the measure
of R&D expenditure to show the validity desired. Moreover,
the R&D measure is used in the discussion below as a proxy
for the level of technological change.

In sum, strong support is given for the effect of the
industry level of product differentiation on the level of
acquisition rates, quite independent of any influence of
parent size.

Concentration. The evidence of a weak negative correlation between concentration and the rate of acquisition appears
to be consistent with the expected hypothesis that target
industries ought to show higher rates of acquisition the lower
the concentration level. The rest relates more to the target
industry hypothesis than to the source industry hypothesis
because of the way acquisition rates were measured. Average

acquisition rates were based on groupings according to the
industry of the subsidiary. Thus the average acquisition rate
is based on the industries which are attracting acquisitions
from parent firms and such industries are expected to be less
concentrated than the industries of the parent firm. If the
average acquisition rate were measured by reference to
groupings of parents by SIC categories, the opposite sign
would be expected for the correlation coefficient. Industry
concentration ratios were obtained from the publication,
Concentration Ratios in Manufacturing Industry, 1963,[2] for
both the eight-firm and four-firm levels. Concentration
ratios were aggregated from the four-digit SIC level to the
three-digit SIC level using the value of U.S. shipments for
each industry as a weighting factor. Certain adjustments were
also made to concentration ratios to eliminate selected four-
digit SIC industries in which U.S. multinationals did not make
foreign investments from the calculations of the concentration
ratios at the three-digit SIC level.[3]

The tests would appear to indicate, from the rough level
of aggregation, that acquisition rates are inversely related
to concentration levels. Using the refinement of adjusting
the concentration ratios to reflect only those industries in
which direct investments occurred, the inverse relationship
appears much weaker than was the case using the unadjusted
concentration ratios, as shown in Table 8-3, for the 3-digit
SIC level. Similar tests on the 2-digit SIC level showed a
-.16 correlation between the industry rate of acquisition and
the eight-firm concentration level.

<u>Industry Stability: The Flow of New Entrants</u>. The
higher the percentage of parent firms that manufactured overseas prior to 1946, the less would be the expected post-war
efforts by industry competitors to match each others moves
in rapid succession--Knickerbocker found this to be the case.[4]
Similarly the rate of acquisition was expected to show a
negative correlation with the percentage of parent firms
within a given industry that manufactured overseas prior to
1946. As hypothesized, a negative correlation of -.21
(see Table 8-3) was found, indicating that for those industries in which most parent firms waited until after 1946 to
move overseas, the use of acquisitions was more frequent than
in industries where most firms had already made their first
investment. This is not to say that the latter group subsequently made fewer total investments in the post-war period--
only that the percentage of acquisitions was lower.

    <u>Industry Stability and Economic Disturbance</u>. Gort
used an R&D measure (ratio of technical personnel to total
employment) as an indication of an industry's level of technological change--and hence of its relative level of economic
disturbance. He found a strong positive correlation with
merger rates (+.74).[5] A slightly different measure, a ratio
of R&D expenditures to sales, showed a strong correlation
with acquisition rates at the 2-digit SIC industry level of
.47. The R&D expenditures/sales figures were also taken from
<u>News Front</u>, March 1966. This relationship may be interpreted
as suggesting that technological change may in fact induce a
higher rate of acquisition. However, since R&D expenditures
may also contribute to higher levels of product differentiation,

the R&D/sales ratio may not simply be reflecting levels of
economic disturbance.

A slightly less consistent picture of the effect of
R&D emerges when parent firms are segregated according to their
level of R&D intensity. As is shown in Table 8-6, there is a
rather weak relationship between the percentage of acquisitions
and parent R&D intensity. Furthermore, as the R&D/sales ratio
is only weakly correlated with parent size -.08 (see Table 8-2),
there is no bias introduced from parent size.

Human Capital Intensity. A final argument that might be
considered in parallel with the product differentiation hypothesis
relates to the entrepreneurial resources of U.S. multinationals.
If U.S. firms possess excess capacity in highly skilled talent
that can be transferred overseas not only for foreign direct
investments,[6] but perhaps for acquisitions. Another question
that can be raised, however, is whether the opportunity cost
of these resources is greater abroad or in the United States,
since diversification in the domestic market would be an alternative outlet for such excess resources.[7] Nevertheless, it
would appear that firms with excesses of such human capital would,
in seeking outlets for such resources, find acquisitions attractive because of the complementary skills in the acquired firm
and the lower risk of entry.

As a rough measure of these firm-specific skills, the
average compensation per employee might serve if it can be
assumed that variations in firm's pay scales are related to
the differences in the level of human capital required. As

Table 8-6

Percentage of Acquisitions and the R&D Intensity of the Parent*

Level of Parent R&D Intensity	Percentage of Acquisitions During the Period in which Subsidiary Began Manufacturing		
	Pre-1946	1946-1957	1958-1967
Total Foreign Subsidiaries Outside U.S. & Canada			
Low R&D Intensity	22.	36.	47.
High R&D Intensity	39.	29.	42.
Subsidiaries Located in Europe Only			
Low R&D Intensity	24.	33.	55.
High R&D Intensity	44.	39.	50.
Subsidiaries Located in LDC's Only			
Low R&D Intensity	20.	36.	34.
High R&D Intensity	41.	23.	34.

*
R&D Intensity is defined as the ratio of R&D expenditures to
sales in 1964.

shown in Table 8-7, human capital intensity does not demonstrate
much relationship at all to the rate of foreign acquisitions.

Summary of the Evidence on Market Structure and Foreign Acquisitions

Product differentiation emerges as the major industry
variable to affect acquisition rates. The ability of acquisitions to increase the utilization of highly developed parent
market skills and as well to reduce the risk of surmounting
the high barriers to entry into new markets is given support
by the strong correlation between the rate of acquisition and
the level of product differentiation.

The concept that industry instability contributes to
higher acquisition rates was given support, although rather
weak. Economies of scale as a motivation for acquisitions
was rejected by the evidence.

Table 8-7

Percentage of Acquisitions and Human Capital Intensity
of the Parent*

Level of Parent Human Capital Intensity	Percentage of Acquisitions During Period in which Subsidiary Began Manufacturing		
	Pre-1946	1946-1957	1958-1967
Total Foreign Subsidiaries Outside U.S. & Canada			
Low Intensity	27.	35.	43.
High Intensity	29.	33.	44.
Subsidiaries Located in Europe Only			
Low Intensity	34.	41.	52.
High Intensity	35.	37.	50.
Subsidiaries Located in LDC's Only			
Low Intensity	17.	27.	30.
High Intensity	23.	32.	37.

*Human capital intensity is based on the average compensation per employee in 1966.

FOOTNOTES TO CHAPTER VIII

1
U.S. Department of Commerce, Bureau of the Census, 1963
Census of Manufacturers, Vol. II, Industry Statistics.

2
U.S. Senate, Subcommittee on Antitrust and Monopoly of the
Committee of the Judiciary, Concentration Ratios in
Manufacturing Industry, 1963, 89th Congress, 2nd session,
1966.

3
The concentration ratios used were ones calculated as
described above by F. T. Knickerbocker in Oligopolistic
Reaction and Multinational Enterprise, op. cit., pp. 213-218.

4
Ibid.

5
M. Gort, "An Economic Disturbance Theory of Mergers,"
Quarterly Journal of Economics, pp. 624-642.

6
An argument for a correlation of skill levels and foreign
direct investment is made in R. E. Caves, "Cause of Direct
Investment: Foreign Firms' Shares in Canadian and United
Kingdom Manufacturing Industries," Review of Economics
and Statistics, February 1975, p. 283.

7
This issue is raised in T. Horst, At Home Abroad: A Study
of the Domestic and Foreign Operations of the American
Food-Processing Industry (Cambridge: Ballinger, 1974).

IX. Host Country Characteristics

Acquisition activity among foreign subsidiaries of U.S. multinationals has varied significantly across countries. An indication of the range of acquisition activity--both in terms of absolute numbers and percentages of acquisitions--for selected countries is demonstrated in Table 9-1 . Size of the host country market and its rate of growth appear to be major explanatory factors of acquisition activity. Unique factors such as small "cultural" distance from the United States or tough legal constraints also appear to have an effect on acquisition rates in selected countries. Difficult to determine is what effect variation in industry mix might have on country acquisition rates.

Market Size and Availability. Acquisition rates in a given market would be expected to be influenced by the relative availability of takeover prospects. As the size of the domestic market is highly related to the number of firms operating in each industry, market size would also be expected to relate strongly to numbers of acquisitions. As has been shown by other researchers, market size has exerted a strong pull on the level of foreign direct investment by U.S. firms. Scaperlanda and Mauer found that the size of the market (as measured by Gross Domestic Product (GDP)) was the most significant indicator of the

Table 9-1

Stock of Manufacturing Acquisitions and the Size of Domestic
Markets (GDP at Factor Cost)

Country	# of Acq.	Acq. as % of total subs. (%)	GDP in 1966 Total ($ mil.)	Per capita ($ mil.)
Europe				
France	86	29 .	91,746	1857
Germany	88	42 .	104,400	1750
Italy	60	38 .	54,302	1045
Belgium & Luxemburg	34	39 .	16,685	1692
Netherlands	24	31 .	18,552	1492
United Kingdom	168	47 .	90,857	1669
Switzerland	9	33 .	12,352	2059
Latin America				
Mexico	80	31 .	21,376	520
Argentina	44	41 .	17,359	758
Brazil	40	29 .	22,720	273
Peru	14	30 .	2,997	250
Colombia	21	23 .	5,816	313
Venezuela	20	20 .	8,169	905
Southern Dominions				
South Africa &			1	1
Rhodesia	50	41 .	11,571	596
Australia & New Zealand	71	30 .	28,037	1963
Asia				
Japan	39	27 .	90,822	919
Philippines	11	22 .	8,357	250

1
 South Africa only.

Source: UN Statistical Yearbook, 1968

flow of U.S. direct investment in the EEC (as measured by
the annual change in the book value of U.S. foreign direct
investment).[1] Knickerbocker also found a positive
correlation (+.72) between GDP in selected countries in
1958 and the number of subsidiaries formed by U.S. multinationals during the period 1948-1967.[2] A similar pull
is expected not only for the absolute number of acquisitions per country but also on the rate of acquisitions.
Large numbers of potential acquisition candidates increases
the chances for successful completion of a takeover search.

The argument is also consistent with evidence from
studies of oligopolistic reaction. As is shown in the
latter part of the thesis, acquisition rates tend to rise
where follow-the-leader behavior is strongest. Knickerbocker's studies showed that oligopolistic reaction was
positively related to a number of country characteristics,
one of which was the size of the market.[3] Thus as firms
in oligopolistically-structured industries react strongly
to each other's moves in countries with large markets a
small increase overall on the rate of acquisitions might
be expected.

In the case of very small markets, however, it is
possible that acquisition rates, rather than declining,
might show some upward bias. Because of the limited
availability of firms within each industry in the very
small markets, the potential multinational investor may

find little room for new investment within a given industry.
There may be no good alternatives but to acquire the local
firm in order to get a foothold in the industry, particularly
if the alternative of setting up a subsidiary from scratch
might have an extremely high cost.

Furthermore, for extremely large markets, there may
not be strong ground to expect a rate of acquisition much
higher than for medium-sized markets. Since the very large
markets can support a greater number of plants per industry
than mexium-sized markets, firms with more than one or two
plants in a given market are likely to perceive less risk
in the decision to set up an additional plant than was the
case for the first plant. The need to use acquisitions as
a means of reducing risk may be a less important factor.
Thus, at very large market size, where the leading firms
already have more than a couple of plants, the rate of
acquisitions might be expected to level off.

The evidence gives good support to the expected
positive relationship between rate of acquisition per
country and the size of the host country market. Over
half (56%) of all subsidiaries formed prior to 1968 in
large sized markets (as measured by GNP in 1970 of $100
billion or more) were acquired compared to an acquisition
rate of about 35% among subsidiaries established in small

countries (GNP in 1970 under $1 billion), as shown in
Table 9-2 . A similar pattern was revealed when acquisition rates per country were related to the level of
economic development (as measured by GNP per capita in
1970), as shown in Table 9-3 .

Market Growth. Overseas market growth provides
another significant stimulus to foreign investment. For
the level of acquisition activity it is perhaps even more
important than market size. That U.S. firms should be
attracted by high growth markets whether domestic or
foreign would seem logical; but for the foreign investor
there are additional reasons. Oligopolists may find
domestic markets crowded and growth limited, whereas
overseas markets may provide greater flexibility for
open competition and less constrained market structures.[4]
Moreover, the follow-the-leader behavior of U.S. oligopolists was particularly evident in countries with high
growth rates. Knickerbocker found a correlation between
his index of entry concentration and the growth rate of
GDP over the period 1950-1960 for selected countries of
46.[5] Thus, risk reduction through the use of defensive
investments may also play a factor in increasing the rate
of acquisition for countries with high rates of growth.
The chance of being left out of a growing market is a
risk that firms in major oligopolies are not likely to

Table 9-2

Total Flow of Manufacturing Acquisitions pre-1968
Classified by Size of Domestic Market (in GNP
in 1970) of Subsidiary's Country

GNP in 1970 of Subsidiary's Country	# of Acquisitions formed pre-1968	Acquisitions as % of total subsidiaries formed pre-1968
		(%)
Under $ 1 billion	36	35 ·
$1-$5 billion	95	38 ·
$5-$20 billion	258	36 ·
$20-$100 billion	1155	52 ·
over $100 billion	638	56 ·

Source: J.W. Vaupel and J. P. Curhan, The World's Multinational
Enterprises (Boston: Harvard Business School, 1973), p. 340.

Table 9-3

Total Flow of Manufacturing Acquisitions pre-1968
Classified by Size of Domestic Market (in GNP
per capita in 1970) of Subsidiary's
Country

GNP per capita in 1970 of Subsidiary's Country	# of Acquisitions Formed pre-1968	Acquisitions as % of total subsidiaries formed pre-1968
Under $200	195	44.
$200-$500	225	37.
$500-$1200	294	42.
$1200-$2500	513	51.
Over $2500	954	57.

Source: J.W. Vaupel and J.P. Curhan, The World's Multinational
Enterprises (Boston: Harvard Business School, 1973), p. 3 38.

take lightly. Moves of one firm are likely to be countered
quickly in markets that have the appearance of becoming
steadily larger. In addition, to the extent that economies
of scale play a role in acquisitions a higher rate of foreign
acquisitions would be expected in high growth industries
where the efficiency of the average firm is likely to be
increasing and as well, the average size of the industry
competitor is getting larger in order to generate greater
economies of scale.

Further, firms trying to diversify their foreign
operations have been attracted in particular to high growth
markets. These factors, in addition to the influence of
availability outlined in relation to market size, should
contribute to an increasing use of acquisitions in
countries with rapid growth rates.

Using the average per annum growth rate of GDP over
the years 1950 to 1967 as a measure of country market
growth, and dividing countries into two fairly equal groups,
using 5 percent per annum growth as a cutpoint, higher
growth rate countries showed a fairly consistent pattern
of higher rates of acquisition over the period 1946 to
1967, shown in Table 9-4 . The countries included in this
analysis attracted about 85% of all foreign subsidiaries
of U.S. firms established between 1946 and 1967. A more
detailed breakdown of the countries comprising this

Table 9-4

Percentage of Acquisition Among Foreign Manufacturing
Subsidiaries Classified According to the Growth
Rate of the Country of Subsidiary's Location

(16 major countries)

Average Per Annum Growth Rate of GDP over Period 1950 to 1967 for Country of Subsidiary's Location	Percentage of Acquisitions for the Period in which Subsidiary Began Manufacturing			
	Pre-1946	1946-1957	1958-1967	1946-1967
Greater or Equal to 5%	30.	40.	56.	51.
Less than 5%	31.	32.	51.	46.

analysis (excluding Japan) is shown in Table 9-5 . .

   Location and Cultural Distance. The distance of
markets from the United States can have effects other
than that normally factored into transportation cost.
Physical as well as "cultural" distance influence the
perceived level of risk in foreign investment. Lower
level of risk has played a role in attracting a higher
rate of investment to markets closer in distance and
nearer in "cultural" similarity to the United States
compared to investment levels elsewhere. Consistent with
this was the observation earlier in the study that small
firms had a tendency to acquire more frequently in countries
such as the United Kingdom, Mexico, and Canada, than did
large firms. Investments in these three countries by small
firms amounted to close to 30% of all foreign subsidiaries
over the period from 1958 to 1967. A somewhat similar overall
pattern of higher acquisition rates for countries with
small "cultural" and physical distance is revealed in
Table 9-5 . Referring to the selected list of countries
showing the numbers of acquisitions that were made during
both the 1946-1957 and 1958-1967 periods, the four countries that were among the first five in rank order in
terms of rate of acquisition for both periods were:
Canada, United Kingdom, Mexico and Australia-New Zealand.

Table 9-5

Flow of Manufacturing Acquisitions and Growth Rates of GDP
at Factor Cost

Country	Acquisitions During 1946-1957			Acquisitions During 1958-1967		
	# of Acq.	Acq. as % of total subs.	Growth in GDP at factor cost 1950-60	# of Acq.	Acq. as% of total subs.	Growth in GDP at factor cost 1960-67
	(#)	(%)	(% p.a.)	(#)	(%)	(% p.a.)
Canada	108	53.	4.3	227	73 .	5.7
Europe						
France	13	34.	4.5	126	59 .	5.3
Germany	27	51.	7.7	97	53 .	4.3
Italy	10	29.	5.3	85	52 .	4.7
Belgium & Luxemburg	3	27.	2.6	45	52 .	4.7
Netherlands*	4	22.	4.6	32	44 .	4.8
United Kingdom	40	40.	2.4	180	66 .	2.9
Switzerland*	0	00.	4.2	12	44 .	4.2
Latin America						
Mexico	31	34.	6.3	116	54 .	6.7
Argentina	13	38.	3.4	42	53 .	2.8
Brazil	19	27.	5.7	43	46 .	3.9
Peru	5	33.	4.7	11	41 .	6.7
Colombia	10	34.	4.6	31	41 .	
Venezuela	8	19.	8.5	25	28 .	5.0
Southern Dominions						
South Africa & Rhodesia*	7	25.	4.4	57	59 .	6.5
Australia & New Zealand*	24	41.	4.0	93	46 .	4.9
Asia						
Japan*	11	42.	8.8	35	29 .	9.6
Philippines	2	10.	6.8	11	35 .	5.7

*
GDP at market prices

Source: UN Statistical Yearbook, 1968

Legal Constraints. A final note should be made concerning the effect on acquisition rates of government
policies toward takeovers. Government policies that
reduce the availability of local acquisition prospects or
increase the riskiness to a foreign firm considering a
local acquisition, may also affect the percentage of
acquisitions observed in various countries. Policies have
been instituted by a number of countries (Japan, for
example) restricting the takeovers of local firms in many
industries. Other countries have instituted criteria for
screening acquisition possibilities (as in Canada and
Australia) to determine whether such takeovers are in the
"best interest" of the host country. These legal constraints
may have important effects on reducing the availability of
acquisition prospects. Even if such laws do not screen out
all available firms, those firms that qualify as prospects
may be limited in number, which may encourage foreigners to
form new subsidiaries instead of making acquisitions.

Legislation can also have the effect of increasing
the riskiness of acquisition prospects to the point that
the projected income streams are discounted to unattractive
levels. The possibility of extended delays in administrative
approvals and the fear of future legislative changes are
examples of such potential risk.

That such policies have had an effect on acquisition
rates is hard to prove. Many countries have introduced
policies over periods too recent to be captured by the
data, as for example in Canada. Countries with long
standing barriers to acquisitions have been able to force
companies to start a larger percentage of new subsidiaries
from scratch. A case in point is Japan where acquisition
rates among foreign subsidiaries formed by U.S. parent
firms prior to 1968 have been held to below the 30% level,
one of the lowest in the world.

Host Country Versus Parent and Industry Effects on
Acquisition Rates. In discussing the expected effect of
host country characteristics on acquisition rates, it should
be noted that there are likely interrelationships between
host country characteristics and various parent and industry
characteristics discussed earlier. For example, large firms
are typically spread out over many countries while small
firms tend to be somewhat more concentrated over a limited
number of major developed countries. If there were to be
fairly equal distribution of investments on a geographical
basis among firms of similar size, then differences between
groups of countries may be relevant to explaining the
differences in acquisition rates observed for differences
in the size of parent firms.

Similarly, country effects may have some importance for comparisons of acquisition rates among industries. To the extent that industries tend to have differing distributions of subsidiaries among foreign countries, specific country characteristics may influence industry acquisition rates. The reverse may also be true. Patterns of acquisitions in host countries may partially reflect the different industry mix in each country. For example, if it were found that certain industries, having low rates of acquisition, tended to invest more heavily in less-developed countries, then the lower acquisition rates observed in these countries might have an alternate explanation from the one discussed above.

While recognizing the possibility of such bias, no patterns of bias were observed consistently to pose a major challenge to the conclusions above. There would appear, however, room for continued research in this area, perhaps using regression models, to help sort out interrelationships between the effects of parent, industry, and country characteristics on acquisition rates.

FOOTNOTES TO CHAPTER IX

1
 A. E. Scaperlanda and L. J. Mauer, "The Determinants of U.S.
Direct Investment in the EEC," American Economic Review.

2
 Knickerbocker, Oligopolist Reaction and the Multinational
Enterprise (Boston: Harvard Business School, 1973), p. 173.

3
 Ibid., p. 171.

4
 Bela Balassa, "American Direct Investment in the Common
Market," Banca Nazionale del Lavoro Quarterly Review, June
1966, pp. 121-246.

5
 Knickerbocker, op. cit., p. 176.

6
 An argument for a correlation of skill levels and foreign
direct investment is made in R. E. Caves, "Causes of Direct
Investment: Foreign Firms' Shares in Canadian and United
Kingdom Manufacturing Industries," Review of Economics and
Statistics, February 1975, p. 283.

7
 This issue is raised in T. Horst, At Home Abroad: A Study
of the Domestic and Foreign Operations of the American
Food-Processing Industry (Cambridge: Ballinger, 1974).

X. Defensive Investment - A Stimulant for Acquisition

As a tool to reduce uncertainty, acquisitions have had an important role. Conditions that give rise to uncertainty appear to have stimulated a shift to greater use of acquisitions by multinationals. Periods of rapid change within an industry are likely to be accompanied by rising uncertainty and greater use of acquisitions. The periods of follow-the-leader behavior that have been shown to be characteristic of some periods of foreign investment activities of U.S. multinationals are prime candidates to satisfy the joint conditions of high uncertainty and a shift to acquisitions.

Special attention has been given to these periods of defensive investment. Unusually high frequency of foreign entry has been observed over short periods of time in selected industries and countries.[1] The occurrence of the pattern of oligopolistic reaction has been explained to some extent as a method of risk minimization on the part of multinationals. As risk minimization and the use of acquisitions have been shown to be close partners, the expectation was strong that use of acquisitions would increase during periods of defensive investments.

Earlier discussion of acquisition theory provides ground for this expectation. Viewed first from the context

of the profit maximizing firm, acquisitions are likely to
be used in the process of making defensive investments
primarily for two reasons: ability to reduce risk and
capacity to utilize complementary resources. Both are
significant factors in the follow-the-leader investment
decision.

Reduction of Risk. The decision to invest for defensive purposes is made in the context of greater than
normal risk. Critical to the defensive investment decision
is its timing. In an oligopolistic setting, use of a new
competitive practice by a rival firm, if allowed to continue unanswered for a period of time, creates a risk of
shifts in relative positions within an oligopoly. Typical
of such a risk would be a decision by rivals to invest in
a new foreign market. Competing firms in the oligopoly
would subsequently have to choose between alternatives of
reacting quickly to the decision, reacting at some later
date, or not reacting at all.

Not to react at all would create the possibility of
the first investor gradually strengthening its position at
the expense of the rival firms. This could happen in a
number of ways. The direct investor could eventually dis-
place the exports of its rivals. Moreover, the first
investor might acquire new skills in the local market that
were transferable back to the U.S. market, which might lead

to a new domestic competitive advantage. Perhaps even more
likely, the experience gained from the direct investment
might provide a comparative advantage with which to move (and
invest)   in other foreign markets. These benefits could
accrue to the first direct investor, and eventually come at
the expense of its rivals. The risk to the competitors of
not reacting is substantial, and as avoidance of such
potential uncertainty is ingrained in the nature of
oligopolists, it is expected that the competitors would
react with defensive investments of their own in the same
foreign market.

Not to be overlooked, however, is the risk of failure
for the initial investor, as well as for the followers.
Both may find themselves in the possession of poor investments. If the first investor were to suffer a loss, while
at the same time the other competitors were not so exposed,
the direct investor would be more susceptible to future
loss of market share to the other firms. Nevertheless, to
the competitors, the risk of the opposite scenario developing
may be more worrisome than the chance of this benefit.
Moreover, even if all the competitors follow the original
investor into a new foreign market and all suffer losses, at
least the burden is spread across the firms and the
stability of the oligopoly is not as likely to be jeopardized.

Too, even in the event of common loss, the oligopoly may
be able to recover part of the losses through higher
prices.[2]

The timing of the defensive investment is also
critical to the decision. Risk aversion plays an important
role here. A delay in countering the first investor's
move increases the risk that the initial investor might
preempt the market from the competitors. For example, if
marketing and distribution channels are limited in a particular country, the initial investor might be able to tie
up the major channels of distribution and close the market
to subsequent investor. The risk of such developments
might lead rivals to prefer rapid defensive reaction to
the initial investor.

This is where the acquisition plays an important role.
The acquisition may provide immediate production and distribution networks and can reduce uncertainties that might
otherwise be present in a decision to construct a new
plant such as the possibility of delays in construction
or supply problems. An acquisition may, of course, require
a high cash outlay compared to the alternative of construct-
ing a new plant. However, the ability of a defensive
investment to reduce the level of risk of future cash
flows would make it possible for the investor to apply a
lower discount rate to the earnings flows of the acquisi-

tion than for the start up operation. The effect of this
reduction of risk could well make the present value of an
acquisition higher than the alternative of starting a new
subsidiary from scratch despite the larger initial cash
payment.

Complementarity of Resources. While reduction of risk
appears to be the strongest motivation for using acquisitions in the follow-the-leader setting, the possibility
for achieving a higher level of complementarity of
resources may also be significant. Complementarity, however,
is not as useful a factor in explaining the need for
urgency in the defensive investment decision as is the
reduction of risk argument. Nevertheless, it may help
explain defensive investments that result from concern
about potential for opportunity loss due to a firm's
inability to maximize its world-wide return on investment.
In particular, the return on investment in intangible
assets (such as organizational abilities and talented
management) may depend on spreading these skills over new
and growing foreign markets.

Maximizing world-wide returns involves maximizing the
returns on the most productive assets the firm has at its
control. For a multinational firm, among these assets
may be the unique set of skills which, in fact, may have
provided the firm's comparative advantage for entering

foreign markets in the first place, such as excellence in R&D or a superior marketing ability. Each firm has a limited set of skills, some of which it may use to exploit new markets. With the development of these skills often regarded as a sunk cost, there may be a low marginal cost for deploying them in new markets. Moreover, if these skills are at the core of factors that generate returns for the multinational firm and if foreign moves by competing firms threaten to reduce the potential markets for these skills, the acquisition may provide a channel for insuring that further returns are generated from these unique skills. A defensive acquisition may allow a multinational firm a means by which return of the firm's assets can be increased.

Growth Maximization. Defensive acquisition may be attractive for additional reasons to growth maximizing firms. This is not to exclude the growth maximizer from using defensive acquisitions to reduce overall risk or to achieve complementarity of resources. These firms may even more jealously be on guard to protect potential markets for foreign growth from being eroded. As expansion proceeds from the domestic market to foreign countries, threats that competitors might preempt growth areas are likely to be met with quick retaliation. Emphasis on maximizing growth rather than profitability is also likely

to result in a lowering of the target discount rates
required for new investment. Defensive investments may
be a particularly good case in point. As the discount rate
becomes lower, acquisitions take on greater attraction
relative to internal expansion. Thus, growth maximizing
firms, even more so than profit maximizers, may turn to
acquisitions during periods of oligopolistic reaction.

Divergence in Evaluation. The likelihood of higher
rates of acquisition occurring during periods of defensive
reaction is also consistent with the economic disturbance
theory of acquisitions. The economic disturbance theory
would expect an increase in acquisitions during periods of
rapid change in the economic or technological environment.
During periods of economic or technological disturbances,
estimates of future earnings flows are subject to increasing
uncertainty. Greater variance in present values are to be
expected from potential buyers and sellers. Thus, with
higher random variances in evaluation, the resulting
randomly generated increase in the number of buyers with
offers higher than sellers' demands is expected to make
possible greater numbers of acquisitions.

The heavy bunching of defensive investments observed
in many foreign industries would appear to have taken place
during periods of economic disturbance. Motivating the
initial foreign investor must have been events sufficient

to induce others in the oligopoly to follow. Underlying
economic disturbances would be likely to cause higher
acquisition activity during periods of bunching because of
the induced divergences in the evaluation process of buyers
and sellers.

In summary, it would appear that defensive investments
are undertaken largely to reduce the uncertainty that might
result if the moves of a competitor into a new foreign
market were not countered. Reduction of uncertainty would
appear to be accomplished better through acquisition of a
foreign subsidiary as compared to alternative investment
choices. The acquisition provides a quicker presence in
the market, gives more ready access to channels of sourcing
and distribution, reduces the probability that the competitor may pre-empt the local market, and allows a firm's
critical skills to be directed toward achieving the highest
returns. In this context, a preference for acquisitions
would appear sensible for firms making foreign investments
for defensive purposes.

Indeed, consistent with this expectation, a noticeable
increase in the frequency of acquisitions was observed
among the foreign investments of U.S. multinational firms
that took place during periods of concentrated bunching of
subsidiaries at the time of entry in foreign markets. The
methodology employed in identifying these periods of

defensive investments is discussed in Chapter XI .
Evidence of the consistent pattern of higher acquisition
rates observed during periods of bunching is presented in
Chapter XI . Moreover, the effect on acquisition activity
of entry concentration and other market characteristics are
taken up in Chapter XII.

FOOTNOTES TO CHAPTER X

1
 F.T. Knickerbocker, Oligopolistic Reaction and Multinational
Enterprise (Boston: Division of Research, Harvard Business
School, 1973).

2
 This concept is discussed in Raymond Vernon, Manager in
the International Economy (Englewood Cliffs: Prentice-Hall,
1972), Chapter 10.

XI.   Acquisition Activity and the Bunching of

Subsidiaries at Entry

Acquisitions have played an active role in the defensive investment strategies of U.S. multinational firms.
During periods in which follow-the-leader behavior was
observed, there was, as expected, clear evidence of an
increase in the rate of acquisitions for a majority of
3-digit SIC industries examined.

Reaching these conclusions required a measure that
could be used to identify periods of bunching. While the
measure used was designed to be similar to that used in
other studies,[1] it is necessary to examine the methodology
before discussing the results.

Methodology of Defining the Bunching Period

A measure was developed in order to test the major
hypotheses relating to the frequency of entry of subsidiaries by acquisitions during periods of oligopolistic
reaction, i.e., periods of highly concentrated bunching at
entry of subsidiaries in the same industry and the same
country over a short time span. In particular, the
measure needed to provide a comparison of the frequency
of acquisitions during such periods of bunching at entry
with the frequency of acquisitions in periods where there
was little bunching at entry. The measure of bunching activity developed was based on that used by Knickerbocker

in other tests of oligopolistic reaction. New measures
that were appropriate for testing hypotheses about acquisitions were generated from the measure of bunching.

Identification of the Period of Bunching. The
pattern of oligopolistic reaction among competing multinationals is said to have occurred when a new foreign
investment by one firm stimulates subsequent foreign investments by one or more competitors. The identification of a
sequence of such investments over a short period of time
is regarded as evidence that some interaction has occurred
between different parent firms. The period during which
interactions were observed is referred to as the period of
bunching. Evidence of interaction has been found consistently
during periods when competing firms in oligopolistic industries imitate each other's moves into new markets for
defensive purposes.[2]

Working from this generalized notion of when interactions occur, a more specific set of rules were laid out
to identify the period of bunching in the data. Bunching
of subsidiaries at entry was defined to have occurred when
two or more U.S. parent firms enter the same industry in
the same country with a given period of time. The
appearance of two or more subsidiaries under such conditions is called an interaction. As industries were defined
according to a 3-digit SIC classification system, an

interaction was recorded only if two or more subsidiaries
entered the same 3-digit industry. Limiting the definition
of an interaction to only within single industries may
appear somewhat confining, as it is possible to suggest
examples of interactions taking place across 3-digit SIC
boundaries--such as an investment by one firm in chemicals
being made as a counter to a competitor's investment in
petrochemicals. However, it would have been rather compli-
cated to identify this kind of interaction in the size of
the data base used in this study. The amount of interactions eliminated by this assumption are estimated to be
small compared to the number occurring within the 3-digit
categories.

An assumption of similar import was that interactions
can take place only within the same countries. This was
justified largely on the grounds that interactions in a
given industry were often concentrated during different
time periods in different countries. The factors that
stimulated a move into one country (such as tariff reduc-
tions, etc.) were likely to be unique to that country at
a particular time. Movements into the same industry in
another country, even if induced by similar factors, would
not necessarily occur at the same time. A major exception
to this logic comes from the investment activities
following the formation of the EEC, where investment in one

country could serve as an offset to a competitor's move into another EEC country. Even for this case, only the last few years of data may have been affected. In any case, there was no attempt made to account for interactions across borders.

The definition of what constituted an interaction also required a limitation for the time interval allowable between the entry dates of two interacting subsidiaries. The interval had to be long enough to include the time lag between the movement of one firm and the response of competitors, and also allow for the possibility of a sequence of firms following each other. Defining the interval to be too long, however, would run a risk of including subsidiaries formed for reasons other than the follow-the-leader motive. A time span of three years seemed to be at least a minimum interval--and seven years a maximum--to capture the responses of competitors to the movement of the initial firm. Rather than arbitrarily selecting one interval separate measures of 3, 5, and 7 years were used in the determination of interactions.

Using these rules, the number of interactions were calculated for each country in each 3-digit SIC industry. This was accomplished by scanning an array that included all subsidiaries that ever produced in each 3-digit SIC industry at the time of entry. The array for each 3-digit

SIC industry was broken down by country groups and within
each country the subsidiaries were listed sequentially by
date of entry. By scanning each country, it was possible
to select the appropriate 3, 5, and 7 year periods of time
during which there was the highest concentration of
entrants of new subsidiaries. The count of subsidiaries
selected within the time interval of greatest bunching
represented the number of interactions.

A Measure for Bunching Activity. Once the number of
interactions had been determined for each country within
each industry, it was possible to construct a summary
measure that would represent the overall magnitude of
bunching activity for each 3-digit SIC industry. A total
of the number of interactions for each industry was obtained
by summing the interactions over all countries. The total
number of interactions for each industry was normalized by
the total number of subsidiaries in each industry, giving
a measure of bunching activity for each industry that could
be compared with other industries. A high measure for a
given industry would indicate that subsidiaries entered the
industry in a highly bunched fashion. A low measure would
indicate that subsidiaries had entered in a fairly gradual
fashion over time.

A Measure for Acquisition Activity. The next step was
to create for each industry a measure that would allow a
comparison of the acquisition activity within the
bunching period with the acquisition activity outside the
bunching period. Calculation of acquisition activity
within the period of bunching followed a procedure similar
to the calculation of the number of interactions. Going
back to the period of bunching for each 3-digit SIC
industry in each country, the number of acquisitions and
the total number of interactions that occurred during the
bunching period were recorded. These numbers were then
summed over all countries for each 3-digit SIC industry.
The percentage of acquisitions within the period of
bunching for each 3-digit SIC industry was obtained by
dividing the total number of acquisitions by the total
number of interactions.

For purposes of comparison, a similar calculation was
made of the percentage of acquisitions that occurred
outside the period of bunching. To determine this measure
for each industry, all subsidiaries that were classified
as interactions in each country were excluded. Then,
summing up the remaining subsidiaries in each industry
across all countries gave both the total number of acquisitions and the total number of subsidiaries recorded outside
the bunching period. The ratio of these two numbers gave
the percentage of acquisitions that occurred outside the

period of greatest bunching.

    <u>Sample Calculations</u>. Data from an actual 3-digit
SIC industry can be used to illustrate the calculation of
the variables outlined above. A list of all subsidiaries
formed in SIC 384 (Medical Instruments and Supplies)
between the years 1948 to 1968 and located within a sample
of 23 major countries is shown in Table 11-1 . (A discussion
of the choice of the time period, list of countries, and
other assumptions used in the analysis of defensive acquisitions is detailed in Chapter II).

    Within each country the subsidiaries are ordered
sequentially by date of entry and are identified according
to method of entry and name of parent. The time span
chosen for the calculation of the period of bunching is
5 years. The five year period during which the greatest
number of subsidiaries entered the 3-digit SIC industry
is identified for each country.

    Having identified the periods of bunching for each
country, the totals can be summed to obtain the industry
statistics. Table 12-2 presents these summary statistics
and calculates the value for a number of frequently
referred to variables.

Table 11-1

Example of Calculation of Period of Bunching (PoB) for 5-Year Span

Industry: SIC 384: Medical Instruments and Supplies

Country	Date of Entry	Acquisitions (Otherwise Formations)	Parent	5-Year PoB	Subsidiaries		Acquisitions	
					Within PoB	Outside PoB	Within PoB	Outside PoB
Australia	61	A	X					
	66		Y		0	2	0	1
Brazil	59		Z					
	66	A	Y	)				
	66		Y	)				
	66	A	Y	)				
	67	A	W	)	4	1	3	0
France	61	A	X					
	61		X					
	66	A	V	)				
	66	A	Y	)				
	66	A	Y	)	3	2	3	1
Germany	56	A	X					
	60	A	U					
	65	A	T	)				
	66	A	T	)				
	66	A	Y	)	3	2	3	2
Italy	63		Z	)				
	64	A	V	)				
	64		X	)				
	65		X	)	4	0	1	0
Netherlands	62	A	X	)				
	64		Z	)	2	0	1	0
U.K.	48		X					
	60	A	S					
	60	A	X					
	62	A	R	)				
	62		Z	)				
	66	A	Y	)				
	66	A	Y	)				
	67	A	W		4	4	3	3
Total	31	21			20	11	14	7

Table 11-2

Example of Calculation of Measures of Acquisition Activity

Industry: SIC 384: Medical Instruments & Supplies

Country	Subsidiaries			Acquisitions		
	Total	Within Period of Bunching	Outside Period of Bunching	Total	Within Period of Bunching	Outside Period of Bunching
Australia	2	0	2	1	0	1
Brazil	5	4	1	3	3	0
France	5	3	2	4	3	1
Germany	5	3	2	5	3	2
Italy	4	4	0	1	1	0
The Netherlands	2	2	0	1	1	0
U.K.	8	4	4	6	3	3
Total	31	20	11	21	14	7

#	Variable	Definition of Variable	Ratio	Value
1.	Entry Concentration Index	$\dfrac{\text{\# subsidiaries WITHIN period of bunching}}{\text{Total \# Subsidiaries}}$	$\dfrac{20}{31}$	.645
2.	Acquisition Concentration Index	$\dfrac{\text{\# acquisitions WITHIN period of bunching}}{\text{Total \# acquisitions}}$	$\dfrac{14}{21}$	.667
3.	% Acquisition	$\dfrac{\text{Total \# acquisitions}}{\text{Total \# subsidiaries}}$	$\dfrac{21}{31}$	.677
4.	% Acquisition WITHIN period of bunching	$\dfrac{\text{\# acquisitions WITHIN period of bunching}}{\text{\# subsidiaries WITHIN period of bunching}}$	$\dfrac{14}{20}$	.700
5.	% Acquisition OUTSIDE period of bunching	$\dfrac{\text{\# acquisitions OUTSIDE period of bunching}}{\text{\# subsidiaries OUTSIDE period of bunching}}$	$\dfrac{7}{11}$	.636
6.	Difference in % Acquisition	% acquisition WITHIN period of bunching minus % acquisition OUTSIDE period of bunching	.700 minus .636	.064
7.	Relative Difference in % Acquisition	$\dfrac{\text{Difference in \% acquisition (Variable 6)}}{\text{\% acquisition (Variable 3)}}$	$\dfrac{.064}{.677}$	.095

1. Entry Concentration Index. The total number of interactions (20) divided by the total number of subsidiaries (31) gives the Entry Concentration Index (ECI) for the 3-digit SIC industry (.645). The ECI measure indicates that 65% of all subsidiaries were formed within the 5-year period for this industry.

2. Acquisition Concentration Index. From among subsidiaries in the bunching period that were acquired (14) divided by the number of acquisitions over the entire period from 1948-1967 (21) gives the 5-year Acquisition Concentration Index (ACI) for the 3-digit SIC industry (.667). This shows that two-thirds of all acquisitions were formed within the 5-year period of bunching.

3. Percentage of Acquisitions. The total number of acquisitions (21) divided by the total number of subsidiaries (31) gives the Percentage of Acquisitions in the 3-digit SIC industry (.677). This indicates over two-thirds of the total number of subsidiaries entered the industry by acquisition over the period 1948-1967.

4. Percentage of Acquisitions WITHIN Period of Bunching. The total number of acquisitions that occurred within the 5-year periods of bunching (14) divided by the total number of interactions (20) gives the Percentage of Acquisition within the Period of Bunching for the 3-digit SIC industry (.700). This indicates that 7 out

of 10 subsidiaries that entered during the period of
bunching were acquisitions.

5. Percentage of Acquisitions OUTSIDE Period of
Bunching. The total number of acquisitions that occurred
outside the 5-year period of bunching (7) divided by the
total number of subsidiaries that were not classified as
interactions (11) gives the Percentage of Acquisitions
outside the period of bunching for the 3-digit SIC
industry (.636). For this industry, the percentage of
acquisitions among subsidiaries that entered outside the
period of bunching was smaller than the percentage of
acquisitions among subsidiaries within the period of
bunching.

6. Difference Between the Percentage of Acquisitions
WITHIN the Period of Bunching and the Percentage of
Acquisitions OUTSIDE the Period of Bunching. The difference between the rate of acquisition among subsidiaries
within the period of bunching (.700) and the rate of
acquisitions among subsidiaries outside the period of
bunching (.636) of .064 reveals the absolute magnitude of
increase in acquisition activity that occurred within
the period of bunching.

7. Relative Difference in Percentage of Acquisitions.
The relative magnitude of increase (or decrease) in acquisition activity within the period of bunching (.095) is

obtained by normalizing the difference between acquisition rates _within_ and _outside_ the period of bunching (.064) by the overall percentage of acquisition over the entire 1948-1967 period (.677).

Using these measures of bunching and acquisition activity, it was possible to test whether acquisitions contributed to the ability of U.S. multinationals to implement defensive investment strategies, i.e., that acquisition activity would increase during periods in which follow-the-leader behavior was observed.

Acquisition Activity and Bunching at Entry

Defensive investment appears to have been accomplished with heavy dependence on acquisitions. During periods of follow-the-leader behavior, acquisition rates increased measurably above normal levels in most industries. At the height of the period of bunching at entry, close to two-thirds of all subsidiaries were acquired. For a large group of industries, this represented close to a 50% increase over levels of acquisition activity excluding the bunching period. Moreover, use of acquisitions for defensive reaction allowed firms to achieve rapid response to competitors as evidenced by the fact that acquisition rates were highest over the short bunching periods.

Consistent Pattern Across Industries. For the
majority of industries in which U.S. multinationals
invested abroad, bunching of subsidiaries implied higher
acquisition rates. When bunching was measured over a
3 year span, over 80% of the industries examined showed
an increase in acquisition rate during the bunching
period, as compared to acquisition rates among subsidiaries
outside the bunching period. However, using longer time
spans to measure the period of bunching, there were fewer
industries that exhibited higher acquisition rates within
the bunching period, as shown in Table 11-3. This supports
the notion that acquisition, if used to achieve rapid
entry in response to the moves of competitors would lead
to high concentration at entry over short periods of time.
Since a 3 year period ought to allow time for reactions to
take place through acquisition, it is consistent that
within the period, acquisitions play their most active role.
Going out beyond the 3 year period, other methods of reaction
to competitors become more practicable and thus reduce the
relative need to rely on acquisitions.

Magnitude of Increase in Acquisition Rate. The higher
rate of acquisition within the bunching period was also
significant in its absolute level. Taking the average of
the rates of acquisition for 46 3-digit SIC industries,
acquisition rates within the 3-year period of bunching

Table 11-3

Industries Classified According to Whether the Percentage
of Acquisitions Within the Period of Bunching is Greater
or Lesser than the Percentage of Acquisitions Outside
the Period of Bunching

(46 3-digit SIC Industries)

Industries With:	3 Year Period of Bunching		5 Year Period of Bunching		7 Year Period of Bunching	
	No. of Indus- tries	% of Total	No. of Indus- tries	% of Total	No. of Indus- tries	% of Total
Rate of Acquisi- tion Greater Within Period of Bunching than Outside Period of Bunching	37	81.	29	63.	29	63.
Rate of Acquisi tions Same Within and Outside Period of Bunching	2	4.	2	4.	1	2.
Rate of Acquisi- tion Greater Outside Period of Bunching than Inside Period of Bunching	7	15.	15	33.	16	35.
Total	46	100.	46	100.	46	100.

showed a 26% increase over acquisition rates outside the
period of bunching, as shown in Table 11-4. The magnitude
of this average increase in acquisition rates attests
further to the major role acquisitions appear to have
played in oligopolistic reaction. The same pattern showed
for the average acquisition rates based on the 5 and 7
year periods of bunching although the magnitude of the
difference was relatively lower than during the 3 year
period. This also confirms the earlier conclusion that
the highest level of acquisition activity appears during
the shortest period of bunching. A similar calculation
made on a sample of 22 industries also shows a higher rate
of acquisition activity occurring during the period of
bunching. Here, however, the magnitude of the difference
between the rate of acquisition within and outside the
period of bunching remains fairly constant regardless of
the length of the bunching period. The 22 industry sample
was a subset of the 46 industry sample that contained
industries with somewhat larger numbers of subsidiaries
that were necessary for in subsequent analyses of the
data.

Averaging the rate of increase over a large sample
smoothed over some significant differences among industries.

Table 11-4

Comparison Between the Percentage of Acquisitions
Occurring Within the Period of Bunching (PoB)
and the Percentage of Acquisitions Occurring
Outside the Period of Bunching

	% Acquisitions Occurring Within PoB	% Acquisitions Occurring Outside PoB	% Acq. Within minus % Acq. Outside	% Acq. Within divided by % Act. Outside
For 46 Industry Sample:				
3 year PoB	63.5	50.5	13.0	1.26
5 year PoB	57.7	50.2	7.5	1.15
7 year PoB	56.0	51.2	4.8	1.09
For 22 Industry Sample:				
3 year PoB	61.6	53.0	8.6	1.16
5 year PoB	61.1	51.6	9.5	1.18
7 year PoB	58.5	51.4	7.1	1.14

As indicated earlier, 80% of the industries showed higher rates of acquisition within the 3-year period of bunching than outside the period of bunching. A look at this group of 80% of the 46-industry sample reveals the magnitude of the increase. For the group (of 39 industries) the acquisition rate among bunched subsidiaries was close to 50% higher than the acquisition rate among other subsidiaries, as shown in Table 11-5. The difference was slightly greater for the groups of industries selected similarly for bunching periods of 5 and 7 years duration.

Role of Acquisitions in Short Periods of Bunching. Briefly touched upon earlier was the notion that if firms use acquisitions to counter rapidly the moves of the competitors, then bunching of acquisitions should occur over a relatively short period of time. It has already been noted that acquisitions have generally been higher during the shorter periods of bunching, especially the 3-year span. Further evidence on this point has been obtained by selecting the period of bunching within which each industry registered its highest rate of acquisition. By far largest number of industries reached the highest rate of acquisition within the 3 year period of bunching, as shown in Table 11-6, based on the 46 industry sample. A similar result, although less striking, was evident

Table 11-5

<u>Comparison of Acquisition Rate Within Period of Bunching</u>
<u>to the Acquisition Rate Outside the Period of Bunching</u>
<u>for Selected Industries</u>

(Sample of industries selected on basis that % Acquisition
Within Period of Bunching is <u>Greater</u> than % Acquisition
Outside the Period of Bunching; i.e., includes industries
represented on the first line of Exhibit 11-3)

Period of Bunching (PoB) Used for Selection of Industries According to Criteria Above	% Acq. Within PoB	% Acq. Outside PoB	% Acq. Within minus % Acq. Outside	% Acq. Within divided by % Acq. Outside
3 year PoB (37 industries)	64.	44.	20.	1.45
5 year PoB (29 industries)	64.	42.	22.	1.52
7 year PoB (29 industries)	55.	36.	19.	1.53

Table 11-6

Length of Period of Bunching Within Which Each Industry
Achieved its Maximum Rate of Acquisition

(46 Industries)

Length of Period of Bunching	Number of Industries Achieving Maximum Rate of Acquisition During the Period of Bunching	Percentage of Total
3 years	27	59.
5 years	13	28.
7 years	6	13.
	46	100.

in the 22 industry sample. Some idea of the variation in the rates of acquisition within the period of bunching that occurs across industries is shown in Table 11-7.

Is Bias Possible from the Overall Trend in Acquisitions? With a generally rising trend of acquisitions over much of the 1960's, it might be suggested that this trend alone could account for the differences in acquisition rates between bunched and non-bunched subsidiaries. Obviously, if all the bunched subsidiaries were located at the high end of a generally rising trend line of acquisitions, the overall pattern of acquisitions would be just as relevant an explanation as the oligopolistic reaction model posed. Examination of the bunching periods for each of the 46 industries, however, reveals significant variation in the appearance of bunching periods over time. Moreover, Knickerbocker showed that a model of oligopolistic reaction using a rising trendline as an assumption for the level of foreign investment activity produced significantly different bunching patterns.[3] Thus, it would appear that the possibility of bias in the interpretation of the data was not significantly introduced by the overall trend in acquisition rates. The conclusion stands that acquisitions were used as a primary tool for achieving rapid follow-the-leader investments during critical periods in a majority of industries.

Table 11-7

3-Digit SIC Industries and the Maximum Rate of Acquisition that Occurred
During One of the Three Periods of Bunching

(22 industries)

3-digit SIC	Period of Bunching (PoB) in which Maximum Rate of Acquisition Occurred and Rate of Acquisition for the Period		
	3-year PoB	5-year PoB	7-year PoB
203		.743	
204		.720	
205		.944	
207	.814		
209		.719	
264		.656	
265		.80I	
281	.378		
282	.407		
283			.426
284	.420		
285	.889		
289		.536	
329			.439
349	.558		
353			.442
355	.833		
356	.556		
363	.588		
367	.733		
371		.628	
384			.704
Totals by # of industries	10	8	4
Percentage of total	.45	.36	.19

FOOTNOTES TO CHAPTER XI

[1]
F. T. Knickerbocker, <u>Oligopolistic Reactions and Multinational Enterprise</u> (Boston: Harvard Business School, 1973).

[2]
Ibid.

XII.   Entry Concentration and Defensive Investment

The tendency for firms to use acquisitions more
frequently during periods of follow-the-leader behavior
has been supported by the evidence in the previous chapter
Carrying this notion one step further, industries where
entry concentration is high are expected to turn more
frequently to acquisitions than industries where entry
concentration is low.

The argument builds upon the basis for expecting
oligopolistic reaction in the first place. In the effort
by multinationals to keep on equal footing with each other,
a movement by one firm in a major market area is likely to
stimulate a parallel response by others. This type of
follow-the-leader behavior has explained the rather high
concentration of entry of subsidiaries in given industries
and given countries over short periods of time. A primary
method by which firms can accomplish rapid response to the
competition's moves of competitors is through acquisitions.
Industries that show extremely tight follow-the-leader
behavior are expected to make greater use of acquisitions,
particularly during the bunching period, than industries
where entry is spread out more evenly over time.

The link between bunching at entry and industry
acquisition rates is strongly supported by the data.

The Entry Concentration Index (ECI) was used as the indicator
of the level of bunching at entry. As described in the
previous chapter, the ECI for each industry is calculated
by taking the number of interactions in each country, summing
the interactions over all countries, and dividing by the
total number of subsidiaries in all countries during the
period 1948-1967. Separate ECI's were calculated for each
of the 3, 5, and 7 year time spans for the bunching period.
The level of correlation between the ECI's and the rate of
acquisitions was very strong. The significance of the
coefficient was also extremely high for all three bunching
periods, as shown in Table 12-1. The relationship between the
rate of acquisition and the 3-year ECI was .65 (with a
significance level of .001), slightly lower for the 5-year
ECI .51 (.003), and even higher for the 7-year ECI .77 (.001).
It would thus appear that firms executing strong follow-the-
leader behavior turned frequently to acquisitions, presumably
as a means of achieving rapid entry into new markets to
offset competitive moves of other firms.

Change in Acquisition Rates During Bunching Period and
Entry Concentration. The evidence presented so far has
confirmed the basic notion that in industries where firms
have followed each other's foreign moves with rapid succes-
sion, causing bunching at entry within short periods of
time, the industry wide acquisition rate has systematically

Table   12-1

Correlation Between Entry Concentration Index (ECI)
and Industry-Wide Rate of Acquisition

(22 industries)

Length of Period of Bunching for which ECI is Measured	Pearson Correlation	
	Coefficient	Significance
3-year ECI	.65	(.001)
5-year ECI	.51	(.003)
7-year ECI	.77	(.001)
Average ECI	.73	(.001)

been high. Industry stability would seem to require
capacity for rapid response.

Another dimension of this relationship is suggested
by earlier evidence showing that acquisition rates were
higher within the bunching period than outside the bunching
period. As the need for rapid response is greatest during
the bunching period, acquisitions are more frequently used.
Consistent with this model would be the expectation that
industries with high entry concentration would correspondingly induce a greater increase in acquisition rates within
the bunching period than would industries with low entry
concentration. The more close knit the bunching, the more
the acquisition rate should differ from its normal level.

This hypothesis was tested on the 22 industry sample.
The difference between the acquisition rate within the
period of bunching and the acquisition rate outside the
period of bunching was used as the measure of the increase
in acquisition rate over normal levels. Since this
absolute difference could lead to some distortions due to
differing levels of normal acquisition activity, a measure
of the absolute difference, normalized by the average acquisition rate, was also used--with similar results. The
difference measure was correlated with the ECI.

The results for the 22 industry sample were mixed.
For the 3 year and 5 year periods of bunching, there was a
weak positive correlation between the ECI and the measure of
the difference in acquisition rates, as shown in Table 12-2.
The correlation was negative for the 7 year period of
bunching. Lack of significant positive results suggested
that the influence of entry concentration was not systematic
over all industries, but left open whether the hypothesized
relationship was not valid for selected subpopulations.

Entry Concentration and the Three Year Bunching Period.
If acquisitions were being used because of their ability to
speed up entry, then the role of acquisitions ought to be
captured most effectively within the shortest time
interval--the 3-year period of bunching. While acquisitions
not captured in the 3-year period of bunching may also be
part of the follow-the-leader behavior, a clearer case can
be made that acquisitions occurring within the 3 year
period are more likely to have been made for the purpose of
obtaining rapid entry. Moreover, industries that were more
actively using acquisitions within the 3 year period than
over the 5 or 7 year periods of bunching would appear to
be regarding acquisitions from a more similar viewpoint--
a means to obtain rapid entry. For these reasons industries
that achieved a higher rate of acquisition during the
3-year period of bunching than during the 5 or 7 year

Table 12-2

Correlation of Entry Concentration Index With the
Difference between the Acquisition Rate for
Subsidiaries WITHIN the Period of Bunching
and the Acquisition Rate for Subsidiaries
OUTSIDE the Period of Bunching, for
3, 5, and 7 Year Periods of Bunching

(22 industries)

Difference Between the Acquisition Rate WITHIN the Period of Bunching (PoB) and OUTSIDE PoB for Each Period of Bunching	Entry Concentration Index		
	3 year ECI	5 year ECI	7 year ECI
3 year Period of Bunching	.09		
5 year Period of Bunching		.21	
7 year Period of Bunching			-.21

periods were all grouped together. Thus all industries that
achieved their maximum rates of acquisition during the 5 or
7 year periods of bunching were excluded from this sample.
This grouping presumably aggregated those industries in
which acquisitions were used systematically as a means of
achieving rapid entry. The test for a relationship between
the ECI and the difference in acquisition rates within and
outside the bunching period was rerun on this set of
industries.

The results were strongly supportive of the hypotheses
that the level of entry concentration has an important
influence on the rise in acquisition rates within the
bunching period. The correlation coefficient of .77
(significance of .021) was observed between the ECI and
the measure of acquisition rate differential, see Table 12-3. The
correlation coefficients shown in Table 12-3 were derived
from a rather small sample of 7 industries. By expanding
the number of industries to include others that reasonably
fit the requirement of having the highest acquisition rate
occur in the 3-year bunching period, the sample size was
increased from 7 to 10 industries. The results for this
larger sample were also encouraging. The correlation

Table   12-3

Correlation of Entry Concentration Index (ECI) for
3, 5, and 7 year Periods of Bunching with
Difference in Rates of Acquisition Among
Subsidiaries Within and Subsidiaries
Outside the Period of Bunching, for
3, 5, and 7 year Periods of Bunching

(7 industries)

Difference in Rates of Acquisition	Entry Concentration Index		
	3-year ECI	5-year ECI	7-year ECI
3-year % Difference	.77	.32	.68
5-year % Difference	.92	.49	.74
7-year % Difference	.59	.13	.18

between the 3 year Entry Concentration Index and the difference in the rates of acquisition for the 3 year period
of bunching was .48.

To check for possible bias that might have been introduced from the use of the measure of the absolute
differential in acquisition rates within and outside the
bunching period, a relative measure was also used. The
relative measure was calculated by taking the absolute
difference in the rates of acquisition for the 3 year period
and normalizing it by the industry average rate of acquisition. (See Variable 7 in Table 11-2). The coefficient of
correlation between the 3 year Entry Concentration Index and
the relative difference in rates of acquisition between subsidiaries within and   outside the 3 year period of
bunching was .34.

Other industry groups were constructed by combining
industries that reached the highest rate of acquisition
during the 5 or 7 year period of bunching respectively.
That these groupings did not generate results of much
significance was not too surprising because the rationale such
industry groupings was not particularly strong.

In summary, defensive investments have made active use
of acquisitions. Industries most active in oligopolistic
lock-step behavior have systematically used acquisitions to

a greater extent than other industries. The increased use
of acquisitions during the peak of the short follow-the-
leader periods is closely related to the intensity of
oligopolistic reaction taking place. High entry concentration over short time periods goes hand-in-hand with a
higher rate of acquisition.

XIII. Summary and Implications

Throughout this study the pieces of evidence on acquisitions have been tied to a framework of the multinational firm as an oligopolist, behaving according to some basic notions of the product life cycle model, and using acquisitions as a vehicle for risk reduction and the efficient, speedy transfer of parent resources to the foreign arena. In marked contrast to the overall secular trend of a gradually increasing frequency of acquisitions among new foreign subsidiaries formed in the post-war era, thestudy revealed that the older more experienced multinationals steadily decreased their acquisition activity over time, with the new entrants to the foreign sphere--the smaller inexperienced firms--relying actively on acquisitions. Some of the implications drawn from this evolving process will be explored after the basic evidence has been reviewed.

The Underlying Theory

Among the basic attributes that made acquisitions attractive, it was particularly the ability of the acquisition to help reduce the level of risk and at the same time to serve as a means of obtaining efficient utilization of parent resources in foreign operations that was found to be systematically related to the selection of acquisitions as the method of entry into foreign markets. That

multinational firms inhabited industries typically characterized by the attributes of oligopolies was key to understanding why risk reduction was so important to the foreign
investment decision. The underlying tie between the
behavior of oligopolies and the flow of investments into
foreign markets by U.S.-based multinational firms was
provided by the product life cycle model. Utilizing this
model to identify and explain why periods of time and
characteristics of the participants lead to a preference
for acquisitions constituted the basic objective of this
study.

The Evidence

From the early 1900's to the late 1960's, the
pattern of foreign acquisitions of U.S.-based multinationals
showed a generally rising trend. Within this secular trend
were cyclical peaks and troughs that closely corresponded
with the levels of acquisition activity taking place in the
domestic market. Cutting right through these overall
patterns in acquisition rates, however, were distinctive
influences attributable to the separate impact of parent,
industry, and host country characteristics.

The Primary Influence: Parent Size. The most
remarkable conclusion of the study was that at the same
time that the rate of U.S. corporate acquisitions abroad
was steadily rising in the post-war period, the rate of

acquisitions among larger and more experienced firms was
steadily _falling_! Small firms showed significantly higher
usage of foreign acquisitions in their expansion abroad.
The explanation of this divergent phenomenon was based on
the use of acquisitions as a risk-reducing investment
medium. Large firms, less risk averse in their foreign
investment decisions than small firms, relied less on the
use of acquisitions. Various measures of parent size and
foreign experience produced consistent results: Using
measures of parent sales, length of foreign manufacturing
experience, numberof foreign subsidiaries, and geographic
diversity, the greater the experience of the parent, the
less need there was to turn to acquisitions in foreign
investments. This pattern was observed consistently over
various periods of time. None of the potential sources of
bias in the trends appeared to hold weight.

Acquisitions as a Means to Foreign Diversification.
Acquisitions were also found to be an attractive means for
achieving diversification in foreign operations. The
potential to reduce the risk of entry into new foreign
industries and to provide a quick and efficient transfer of
skills from the parent to the foreign subsidiary appeared
to be underlying determinants. The propensity to use
acquisitions to diversify abroad was evidenced by the fact

that the rate of acquisitions was systematically lower among
subsidiaries in the same 3-digit SIC industry as the
parent's primary 3-digit SIC industry than was the rate of
acquisitions among subsidiaries in industries outside the
primary 3-digit SIC industry of the parent. Product
diversity was also correlated to the use of acquisitions.
Acquisition rates were consistently higher among subsidiaries with parents having greater product diversity.

There was a distinct, but not too lengthy, lag
between the levels of domestic and foreign diversification
respectively. This suggested that the diversification into
various product lines took place first domestically. This
relative timing of the movement to greater levels of
diversity in foreign operations was consistent with the
product life cycle notion that products developed domestically
eventually flow overseas. Like the flow of other products
overseas, the flow of diversified products into foreign
markets followed after their appearance in the domestic
product lines of the parent firms.

The Influence of Industry Characteristics on
Acquisitions. Industry characteristics that lead to a
higher use of acquisitions further supported the notion
that efficiency in the transfer of human skills from the
parent to its foreign operations was closely linked to a
propensity to acquire abroad. Product differentiated

industries, notable not only for high levels of foreign
investment activity but also for an ability to achieve
significant benefits in foreign operations from the
transfer of key skills (largely marketing and distribution)
developed in the domestic market, also showed a systematically
higher use of foreign acquisitions.

Sources of industry instability also appeared to
induce higher acquisition rates. Industries that were
characterized by a rapid inflow of new parent firms into
foreign markets in the post World War II period as well as
industries that showed potential for high levels of technological change (as measured by the R&D intensity of the
industry), tended to make more frequent use of acquisitions.
This pattern would appear to be consistent with the risk-
reducing value of acquisitions and as well with the model
of economic disturbance as a cause of acquisitions.

As a method of achieving economies of scale in
production in foreign operations, little support was given
to the value of acquisitions in this process. Finally, the
notion that the pursuit of monopoly power was an underlying
cause for foreign acquisitions was undermined both by
evidence that U.S. parents appeared to seek significant levels
of diversification in their foreign operations and by the
strong negative relationship observed between industry concentration and industry rates of acquisition.

Host Country Characteristics. Market size as measured by the country's GNP and the growth in market size were found to exert a strong pull on the number as well as the frequency of foreign acquisitions. The availability of acquisition prospects would appear to be a primary influence from both of these characteristics. Rapid market growth may have also contributed to inducing follow-the-leader investment patterns by U.S. firms, which would also have increased the use of acquisitions. Small firms appeared to have been particularly active in foreign investment through acquisitions in countries either close to the United States or where cultural differences were small, suggesting that reduced levels of perceived risk were important factors in both cases.

Defensive Investment. The risk-reducing value of acquisitions was particularly evident in the role that acquisitions played during the periods of follow-the-leader behavior exhibited by U.S. parent firms. During these periods, the rate of acquisition in a large majority of industries rose measurably above levels observed during periods not characterized by the bunching of subsidiaries at entry. Moreover, the industries where entry concentration was high also had high rates of acquisition. Those industries with the most significant increases in acquisition activity during the bunching period also showed the highest intensity of the entry concentration.

This cursory review of the major themes of evidence
sets the stage on which implications can be drawn for
decision-makers.

Acquisition Theory in Perspective

Despite the statistical limitations of the evidence,
the profit-maximizing model of the firm held the most
explanatory value. The most recurrent themes in the role
of acquisitions in the foreign investment process were
associated with aspects of acquisitions based on the theory
of the firm as a profit maximizer. In particular, that an
acquisition could generate higher returns for the combination
of two firms, above the level of returns possible to the
separate firms, was an underlying argument for the complementarity of under-utilized resources in the two firms.
Moreover, the ability of an acquisition to reduce the level
of risk in a foreign investment was related directly to
the effect that risk-reduction has on the discount rate that
the acquiring firm applies to the analysis of the investment.
This argument is also part of the view of acquisitions taken
from the profit maximization model of behavior.

Other motives for acquisitions suggested by the
profit maximization model were found to have little
systematic importance in foreign acquisitions. The effect
of economies of scale in increasing the returns to acquisitions was not ·seen as an important factor in the evidence

relating to overseas activity. Similarly, the monopoly
power motive had little explanatory value in the acquisitions made in foreign markets.

The theory that economic disturbances lead to higher
acquisition rates was also given some support from the
evidence on foreign acquisitions. However, the tests that
would appear to give support to this line of reasoning were
not well defined enough to be distinguishable from tests of
alternative acquisition theories. For instance, the fact
that R&D intensity was correlated positively with acquisition rates could be read as supporting the theory that
rapid technological change was a form of economic disturbance
that would lead to higher rates of acquisitions. However,
R&D intensity could also be read as an indicator of product
differentiation which would lead to acquisitions for a
fundamentally different reason, i.e., the ability to maximize
the returns on underutilized domestic resources. A similar
problem of interpretation was encountered in the other piece
of evidence cited as supporting the economic disturbance
argument: the fact that the rapid inflow of new parent
firms into a number of industries during the post World
War II period was accompanied by high rates of acquisitions.
While this evidence could be consistent with the economic
disturbance model for foreign acquisitions, the same could
be said for the argument that risk-reduction was the factor

operating to make acquisitions attractive during this
period. Despite these problems, there was no evidence
that appeared to be highly inconsistent with the economic
disturbance model, thus lending some credence to its
effect on foreign acquisitions.

The growth maximization theory did not appear to
generate much support. In fact it would appear to run
somewhat counter to some of the conclusions derived from
the influence of parent size on foreign acquisitions. The
growth maximizing theory would tend to argue for a higher
rate of acquisition for large firms that, having exhausted
the opportunities for internal growth, would seek to expand
externally through acquisitions. And although there was a
clear relationship between external expansion through acquisition and diversification, there was no direct link between
diversification and parent size.

The tradeoffs between the various theories of
acquisition and their implications for the foreign investment process could not be refined much further without having
better estimates of data that related specifically to
industry characteristics of the foreign markets.

Policy Implications for Host Countries

To the extent that host country policy makers under-
stand the behavior of multinational firms, the better able
they are to design policies to influence foreign investors

in line with host country objectives. This obvious point
has been used effectively by others for designing foreign
investment codes for host countries, particularly the
LDC's.[4] The patterns of acquisition activity observed in
this study may add other dimensions to the methods host
countries can use to attract the multinational firm.

Competition and Market Structure: Effect on Foreign
Acquisitions and Vice Versa. Among the goals of any foreign
investment code is the maximization of the net benefits
resulting from the entrance of foreigners into the domestic
economy. In the case of acquisitions, however, country codes
often take the form of erecting barriers to acquisitions.
Acquisitions by foreign firms are presumed to lead to
increased levels of industry concentration in local industry
and, thus, possibly resulting in reduced competition.

What this study suggests, however, is that the flow
of foreign acquisitions is typically higher in industries
characterized by low levels of concentration. Entry into
more highly concentrated industries would appear to take
place via de novo investments rather than by acquisition.

This would suggest that the majority of the foreign
acquisitions made by U.S. multinationals would not pose a
threat to host country policies designed to prevent acquisitions in highly concentrated industries and subsequent

foreign dominance in key sectors. In fact, policies designed
specifically to counter the flow of acquisitions into selected
highly concentrated industries would deter only a small
number of acquisition possibilities (although the size of
each such acquisition would likely be large compared to
the average size of foreign acquisitions of U.S. firms).
Such a selective policy of preventing foreign acquisitions
from causing increasing levels of concentration in already
highly concentrated industries would still leave the less
concentrated industries open to foreign acquisitions.

Another general presumption for creating barriers
to foreign acquisitions is that the bundle of skills,
resources, technologies and capital brought into the host
country via the newly formed subsidiary is likely to result
in greater net benefits than were the same investment made
via the acquisition route. What this generalization over-
looks is that such policies might turn away for good certain
types de novo investments that might otherwise have taken
place through acquisition. A particular area where this
might be the case is suggested by the evidence relating to
the investment behavior of small multinational firms. The
heavy dependence that small firms have shown for using
acquisitions as a means of entering into overseas competition

with larger firms may have some important implications for
the structuring of investment codes for foreign acquisitions.

Acquisitions in the Context of Risk-Reducing Incentives.

Various risk-reducing aspects of foreign investment codes have been shown to have particular attraction to
foreign investors. Multinational firms may place a higher
value on factors that reduce the level of perceived risk in
a particular investment decision than on aspects that increase
the level of returns, especially in investment situations
where the level of risk starts out very high, such as may be
the case in various LDC projects. The provision of government loans, creation of infrastructure, erection of factories
and warehouses are but examples of such cost-reducing offerings
by the host countrie as a means of attracting the foreign
investor. It is to be suggested here that there may be ways
that the availability of acquisition prospects may selectively
be used as an alternative risk-reducing tool to attract multinationals, particularly the small firms.

Special Benefits for the First Investor.

As is the
case in some foreign investment codes, the first investor
might be given favorable treatment relative to that of
subsequent investors. Behind such a policy is the notion
that the first investor faces greater risk and may need
special consideration in order to be induced to hurdle the
barriers to foreign investment in the host country. Once

an investor has been attracted, subsequent investors can be
expected to show less hesitation. For one thing, some firms
may feel compelled to match the move of the initiator.
Moreover, the success of an initial investor reduces the
risk parameters perceived by the subsequent investors.
Thus, attracting the first investment may justify special
incentives not offered to others.

A further argument can be advanced that small firms
within a particular industry should be specifically sought
out for such special treatment. Small firms are attractive
to a host country as first investors partly because they
may be easier to negotiate with but also because the
inducements offered may be smaller than would be the case
for larger firms.

Where the evidence from this study bears upon the
analysis is that the small investor is more risk-averse
in its foreign investment decisions than the large investor
and is thus more likely to pay attention to various risk-
reducing tools offered by the host country. One such risk-
reducing factor that might be a very effective way of
inducing a small investor would be to make available a
number of local prospects for acquisition.

Acquisition Filter Rules. A general policy could be
established that to accomplish the purpose of allowing the

small firm to acquire locally early in the game, but preventing the larger followers from using the same method of
entry. An acquisition filter rule that sets a small upper
limit on the size of theacquisitions allowed, might filter
out inquiries from large foreign investors, which are not
likely to be attracted to small acquisition prospects.

A filter that limited the absolute number of acquisitions allowed per industry might also work to stimulate
investment by small firms. The small firm, knowing there
were only a few chances for making acquisitions, might
speed up its decision to invest for fear of being excluded
from the chance to acquire at all.

There may be difficulties, however, in imposing
schemes that may appear to favor a particular subset of
firms. Some countries are reluctant to introduce public
policies with clear favoritism for specific investors.
While this attitude may reduce the potential for policies
that favor the first investor, the same objective could still
be met by imposing one or another form of the filter rules.

Going to the other extreme, rules that impose very
tight restrictions on acquisitions by all foreign investors
may run the risk of excluding the small firms from the
competition. In the long run, this may reduce the level of
competition within particular industries, with potential

detrimental effects on the host country.

     Conclusion. Although the arguments made here have
been along the lines of leaving open the channels for the
foreign investor to enter the host country via the acquisition route, clearly there are arguments for maintaining
tough policies on acquisitions in various circumstances.
The follow-the-leader behavior that has characterized
periods of investment activity of U.S. multinationals, as
noted above, would be expected to continue even in those
countries where acquisitions have been restricted. The
evidence to the contrary, however, would suggest valid
reasons for leaving the borders open selectively to foreign
acquisitions. The potential for beneficial impact on the
host country reflects in part the fact that foreign acquisitions appeared with higher frequency in industries with low
levels of concentration than in the more sensitive highly
concentrated industries. Potential benefits of such policies
might also come not only from the generation of higher levels
of foreign investment but as well from the stimulation of
the local competition that the threat of external entry
may have on existing firms within the host country.

Implications for the Corporate Decision Maker

     The study of the acquisition behavior of U.S.
multinational firms has revealed not only areas of systematic

influence concerning the acquisition decision but also
factors related to the decision-making process itself.
The decision to acquire was consistently related to the
ability of an acquisition to serve as a medium for the
reduction of risk and for the efficient utilization of
complementary resources. The underlying decision-making
process would appear consistent with the notion that
these firms were capable of taking a worldwide view of
their operations and were able to evaluate the marginal
costs and benefits to the system as a whole of investment
decisions relating to separate parts of a widely spread
system. The profit-maximization goal of the firm would
appear to have largely withstood (at least for the acqui-
sition-decision-making process) the potentially offsetting
pull of sub-units to pursue sub-optimal behavior.

Implications for the Foreign Investment Decision:
The Present Value Approach. Although each foreign investment (or acquisition) decision will have its own unique
characteristics, certain elements of systematic importance
should be factored into the acquisition decision. In
estimating the cash flows for the analysis of an acquisition,
the true marginal cost or benefit, to the system as a sholw,
should be assigned to the calculation, rather than the full
cost that may appear in one subunit. Similarly, the discount

rate to be used in a present value calculation should
incorporate the effect that the acquisition has on the
overall level of corporate risk--either by directly
altering the discount rate itself or, if possible, by
altering the cash flows to account for the difference in
level of risk. Failure to adequately account for the
marginal system-wide cash flows or system-wide level of
risk could jeopardize the validity of the decision.

Potential Problem Areas: (1) Consideration of
Dynamic Elements. An overestimation of the advantages of
an acquisition is a possibility particularly when dynamic
elements of an acquisition are neglected. For instance,
evidence from this study would suggest that there is a
risk that an acquisition may stimulate a sequence of follow-
the-leader investments by competitors, which may offset
the expected positive results of an acquisition. The
forecast of future cash flows should factor in some risk
that such a competitive reaction would reduce the potential
for growth in revenues.

(2) Economies of Scale Benefits. Special attention
should be paid to the potential pitfall of projecting
significant benefits from economies of scale resulting from
an acquisition. The lack of systematic evidence in support
of the argument that economies of scale in production can
provide an important basis for motivating acquisitions
should give rise to skepticism when such prospects are
expected. Little scale benefits can be expected from

location-specific additions to existing multiplant operations.

(3) Benefits of Complementarities. Caution should be
exercised in estimating the benefits of complementarity
between parent skills and subsidiary needs. Costs of
modifying parent skills to be adaptable to foreign situations
should be incorporated. Moreover, when many investment
alternatives are competing for the same set of parent skills,
an average cost at the margin must be assigned.

Avoiding Acquisitions through Planning: Anticipating
High-Risk Situations. Alternative means of achieving the
same end (for a lesser cash outlay) may be available if a
firm plans far enough in advance to avoid some of the high-
risk situations that make acquisitions attractive. Acquisitions have been shown to be a preferable investment medium
when conditions of high-risk exist. The example of the
follow-the-leader behavior might lead a firm to acquire into
a foreign market to match quickly the move of a competitor.
However, if forward planning could have identified the
market in question as a favorable location for future investment and, as well, a market in which there was likely to be
potential investment from competitors, a more gradual (and
perhaps less costly) approach might have been designed to
meet the same objective (with a similar end-point level of

risk). Consideration of alternative investment media might
lead to a higher present value; at least the firm would be
exercising a conscious choice not to invest through an
alternative arrangement if it decided to wait for a competitor to invest before following up with an acquisition.

Taking Advantage of High Risk Situations: The Large
Firm. Large firms may have a special advantage over smaller
firms in acting upon certain high risk situations. Investment alternatives with unacceptably high risk to a small
firm may be tolerable to a large firm. As an example, some
countries erect high barriers to foreign acquisitions. The
large firm may be able to invest in such situations with
the expectation of few competitive threats from smaller
firms. These barriers may keep out the smaller firms, while
at the same time creating a protective environment for
existing firms. This could present a potential entry point
for large firms. Thus, a careful review of major country
markets might reveal possibilities for forming new operations
from scratch, with potential for significant long term
rewards.

Implications for the Divestor. The other side of
the acquisition process, the seller, whether it be a U.S.
firm divesting of foreign assets or a foreign firm selling
all or part of its assets, may be able to gain a higher

return by selectively searching for potential buyers. A
higher price would more likely be paid by a firm seeking a
means of reducing risk or trying to take advantage of
complementarities. The seller might be advised to look
first at the medium to smaller sized (as opposed to large
sized) firms from among possible acquirers, i.e., among
firms more likely to place a greater value on the acquisition. Another strategy for a company seeking a U.S. buyer
might be to wait until another U.S. multinational enters
the same industry as the selling firm--either through a
start-up operation or an acquisition of a competitor--
expecting that the subsequent follow-the-leader investment
behavior might generate interest from other U.S. multinationals for making an acquisition and hopefully netting
the seller a higher price.

Longer-Term Acquisition Patterns. Improving the
understanding of the mechanisms that motivate the behavior
of large multinational firms should lead to better forecasts
of the trends of corporate behavior and more efficient
decisions. Long-range strategic planning for an oligopolistic
firm relies heavily on its assumptions of the behavior of
its competitors. An improved understanding of the foreign
acquisition behavior of U.S. multinationals should contribute,
in some part, to the ability of a corporate planner to design

a viable strategy for the firm.

Prospects for Further Research

A logical extension of the examination of foreign acquisitions of U.S.-based multinationals would be a similar study of multinationals based in other countries. Some preliminary evidence suggests that there appear to be some common trends, although a conceptual framework incorporating the effects of differing national origins is clearly lacking.

Foreign-Based Multinationals: Are There Similar Patterns?

To begin with, the basic attributes of acquisitions would not be expected to change. What may signify differences in the behavior of non-U.S.-based firms would be differences in their attitudes toward the key factors that were found to underly the interest of U.S. firms in acquisitions: namely, the desire to avoid risk and the need for a quick and efficient transfer mechanism for parent skills to foreign markets.

One exploratory possibility would be that non-U.S.-based firms may indeed have viewed one of these factors with less importance: the value of acquisitions as a risk-minimization tool. While this study does not try to answer the question, it is known that European firms have typically succeeded in using institutional methods (e.g., cartels) to reduce some risks of foreign investment, at least in the not too distant past.[1] If this attitude, for instance, affected

the perceived need to counter the moves of competitors, particularly where market sharing arrangements are strong, a
lower use of acquisitions might be expected to result.

A passing look at some selected evidence on the
foreign acquisitions of non-U.S.-based multinationals
reveals some similarities to the patterns exhibited by
U.S.-based multinationals. The data is taken from the data
base on non-U.S.-based multinational enterprises developed
under Professor Raymond Vernon's direction at the Harvard
Business School.[2] To start with, the overall rate of acquisition among manufacturing subsidiaries of non-U.S.-based
multinationals was equal to that of a comparably reported
data base of U.S.-based firms, 49 percent. (A larger sample
of non-U.S.-based firms covering a slightly longer period of
time showed an acquisition rate of 55 percent.)

Influence of Parent Size on Acquisition Rates. Similar
patterns are observed between U.S.-based and non-U.S.-based
firms in the effect of parent size on foreign acquisition
rates. The differential effects of parent size on the risk
of foreign investment apparently seems to hold, even though
the overall level of acquisition activity among non-U.S.-
based firms may be different. Smaller firms showed a higher
preference for acquisitions among foreign subsidiaries than
are larger firms, as shown in Table 13-1.

Table 13-1

Percentage of Acquisitions Among Foreign Manufacturing Subsidiaries of Non U.S.-Based Parent Systems Classified by the Size of the Parent (As Measured by Sales in 1970)

Value of Sales of Subsidiary's Parent in 1970	Percentage of Acquisition
$400 - 599 million	60.
$600 - 999 million	56.
$1 - 2 billion	56.
Over $2 billion	48.

Source: J.W. Vaupel and J.P. Curhan, The World's Multinational Enterprises (Boston: Harvard Business School, 1973), p. 350.

Influence of Host Country Size on Acquisition Rates.
The persistent pattern of host country influences on U.S.-
based firms might also expect to hold for the non-U.S.-
based firms. Larger markets would be likely to exert a
strong pull on acquisitions as was the case for U.S. firms.
As shown in Table 13-2, the pattern was more exaggerated
than in the U.S. case with the largest markets attracting
almost twice the rate of acquisitions as the smallest
markets. The same pattern was observed for acquisition
rates ranked by the GNP per capita of the host country.
The rate of growth of foreign markets was not as clearly an
inducement for higher rates of acquisitions as was the case
for the U.S. firms. Perhaps this may have been due to the
fact that the non-U.S.-based firms acquired with great
frequency throughout Europe and North America without special
regard for growth rates. In fact, the existence of the EEC
may have made the question of individual country growth
rates in EEC countries less important during the period
following the formation of the EEC.

National Base of Parent Firms. Differences appear in
rates of acquisition when parent systems are divided according
to national base. Various factors could be operating to cause
such differences, such as country size, country location, and
industry mix, and no attempt is made to distinguish among

Table 13-2

Percentage of Acquisitions Among Foreign Manufacturing Subsidiaries
of Non U.S.-Based Parent Systems Classified by the GNP in
1970 of the Subsidiary's Country

GNP in 1970 of Subsidiary's Country	Percentage of Acquisition
Under $1 billion	36.
$1 - 5 billion	39.
$5 - 20 billion	45.
$20 - 100 billion	58.
Over $100 billion	67.

Source: J.W. Vaupel and J.P. Curhan, The World's Multinational
Enterprises (Boston: Harvard Business School, 1973), p. 339.

them. As shown in Table 13-3, the range in acquisition rates varied from a low of 14% for Japan to a high of 64% for the United Kingdom.

To what extent country characteristics influenced acquisition rates cannot be answered without much analysis. Some possible questions could be raised, such as: could the effective cartelization of Japanese enterprise have had a significant effect in reducing the acquisition rate among the foreign subsidiaries of Japanese firms. Similarly, could the relatively small domestic markets in a country like Belgium have stimulated its firms to acquire more frequently overseas as a risk minimizing tool--noting in this context that Belgium and Luxemburg had higher rates of acquisitions among their foreign subsidiaries than any of the other original six EEC countries.

Tip of the Iceberg. These preliminary views of the relationships between acquisition rates and the behavior of firms of different national origin merely raise a few questions. More careful foundations for hypothesizing about the influences of national origin on multinational firm behavior are being explored with the help of the new data base on the World's Multinational Enterprises.[3] The implications for acquisition behavior should be easier to draw out in the context of these more fundamental inquiries.

Table 13-3

Percentage of Acquisitions Among Manufacturing Subsidiaries
of Non U.S.-Based Parent Systems Classified According
to the National Base of the Subsidiary's Parent
System

National Base of Subsidiary's Parent System	Percentage of Acquisitions Among Total Subsidiaries Formed by Parent Systems	Total Number of Subsidiaries Formed by Parent Systems
United Kingdom	64.	2153
Belgium and Luxemburg	57.	255
The Netherlands	56.	413
Sweden	56.	195
Switzerland	54.	411
Canada	53.	265
Germany	52.	931
France	46.	297
Italy	45.	102
Japan	14.	503

Source: J.W. Vaupel and J.P. Curhan, The World's Multinational
Enterprises (Boston: Harvard Business School, 1973), p. 349.

Other Issues for Further Research. A second area for
continuing research would be to try to measure the separate
weighting of each of the primary factors that influenced
acquisition rates: parent, industry and host country characteristics. This effort would require more detailed
indicators of each of these characteristics, in particular
broken down by 3-digit SIC industry and adjusted for the
appropriate foreign markets of each industry. While the
current study would appear to show that parent size was
the dominant factor, a segregation of the influences would
significantly broaden the application of the results.

FOOTNOTES TO CHAPTER XIII

1
  L. G. Franko, "The Origins of Multinational Manufacturing by
Continental European Firms," Business History Review,
Autumn 1974, pp. 277-302.

2
  Statistical summaries of the data are presented in
J. W. Vaupel and J. P. Curhan, The World's Multinational
Enterprises (Boston: Harvard Business School, 1973).

3
  Ibid.

MULTINATIONAL CORPORATIONS:
Operations and Finance

An Arno Press Collection

Aggarwal, Raj Kumar. **The Management of Foreign Exchange** (Doctoral Dissertation, Kent State University, 1975). Revised edition. 1980

Ahrari, Mohammed E. **The Dynamics of Oil Diplomacy** (Doctoral Dissertation, Southern Illinois University, 1976). 1980

Atkins, Edwin F[arnsworth]. **Sixty Years in Cuba**. 1926

Ayarslan, Solmaz D. **A Dynamic Stochastic Model for Current Asset and Liability Management of a Multinational Corporation** (Doctoral Dissertation, New York University, 1976). 1980

Bassiry, Reza. **Power vs. Profit** (Doctoral Dissertation, The State University of New York at Binghamton, 1977). 1980

Bodinat, Henri de. **Influence in the Multinational Corporation** (Doctoral Dissertation, Harvard University, 1975). 1980

Burgess, Eugene W., and Frederick H. Harbison. **Casa Grace in Peru**. 1954

Chandler, Alfred D., Jr., compiler and editor. **Giant Enterprise**. 1964

Cleveland, Harlan, Gerard J. Mangone, and John Clarke Adams. **The Overseas Americans**. 1960

Daniel, James, editor. **Private Investment**. 1958

Dubin, Michael. **Foreign Acquisitions and the Spread of the Multinational Firm** (Doctoral Dissertation, Harvard University, 1976). 1980

Finnie, David H. **Desert Enterprise**. 1958

Harrington, Fred Harvey. **God, Mammon, and the Japanese**. 1944

Heller, Kenneth Howard. **The Impact of U.S. Income Taxation on the Financing and Earnings Remittance Decisions of U.S.-Based Multinational Firms with Controlled Foreign Corporations** (Doctoral Dissertation, The University of Texas at Austin, 1977). 1980

Jadwani, Hassanand T. **Some Aspects of the Multinational Corporations' Exposure to the Exchange Rate Risk** (Doctoral Dissertation, Harvard University, 1971). 1980

Jeannet, Jean-Pierre. **Transfer of Technology within Multinational Corporations** (Doctoral Dissertation, The University of Massachusetts, 1975). 1980

Konz, Leo Edwin. **The International Transfer of Commerical Technology** (Doctoral Dissertation, The University of Texas at Austin, 1976) 1980

Logar, Cyril M. **Location of Responsibility for Product-Policy Decisions of United States-Based Multinational Firms Manufacturing Consumer Goods** (Doctoral Dissertation, Kent State University, 1975). 1980

Macaluso, Donald G. **The Financial Advantage of Multinational Firms During Tight Credit Periods in Host Countries** (Doctoral Dissertation, New York University, 1975). 1980

Mascarenhas, Oswald A.J. **Towards Measuring the Technological Impact of Multinational Corporations in the Less Developed Countries** (Doctoral Dissertation, The University of Pennsylvania, 1976). 1980

Moneef, Ibrahim A. Al-. **Transfer of Management Technology to Developing Nations** (Doctoral Dissertation, Indiana University, 1977). New introduction by Stanton G. Cort. 1980

Moore, E[lwood] S. **American Influence in Canadian Mining.** 1941

Moore, Russell M. **Multinational Corporations and the Regionalization of the Latin American Automotive Industry** (Doctoral Dissertation, Tufts University, 1969). Revised edition. 1980

O'Connor, Walter F. **An Inquiry into the Foreign Tax Burdens of U.S. Based Multinational Corporations** (Doctoral Dissertation, The City University of New York, 1976). 1980

Persaud, Thakoor. **Conflicts between Multinational Corporations and Less Developed Countries** (Doctoral Dissertation, Texas Tech University, 1976). 1980

Przeworski, Joanne Fox. **The Decline of the Copper Industry in Chile and the Entrance of North American Capital** (Doctoral Dissertation, Washington University, 1978). 1980

Raveed, Sion. **Joint Ventures between U.S. Multinational Firms and Host Governments in Selected Developing Countries** (Doctoral Dissertation, Indiana University, 1976). 1980

Renforth, William, and Sion Raveed. **A Comparative Study of Multinational Corporation Joint International Business Ventures with Family Firm or Non-Family Firm Partners** (Doctoral Dissertation, Indiana University, 1974). Revised edition. 1980

Siddiqi, M. M. Shahid. **Planning and Control of Multinational Marketing Strategy** (Doctoral Dissertation, The University of Pennsylvania, 1976). 1980

Sorey, Gordon Kent. **The Foreign Policy of a Multinational Enterprise** (Doctoral Dissertation, The University of California, Irvine, 1976). 1980

Stanford Research Institute. **Foreign Investment.** 1980

Stopford, John M. **Growth and Organizational Change in the Multinational Firm** (Doctoral Dissertation, Harvard University, 1968). 1980

Toyne, Brian. **Host Country Managers of Multinational Firms** (Doctoral Dissertation, Georgia State University, 1975). 1980

Tsurumi, Yoshihiro. **Technology Transfer and Foreign Trade** (Doctoral Dissertation, Harvard University, 1968). Revised edition. 1980

Wells, Louis T., Jr. **Product Innovation and Directions of International Trade** (Doctoral Dissertation, Harvard University, 1966). 1980